CONTENTS

KU-684-872

1

INTRODUCTION

HOW TO USE THE BOOK

EACH CHAPTER IN this book examines one or more of the central debates relating to the sociology of locality, community and nation. The text is devised for readers with little or no background knowledge in the subject, and there are Study Points and Activities throughout to encourage a consideration of issues raised. You are advised to make use of these and answer them either on paper or in group discussion, a particularly fruitful way of learning; they will assist you to develop the skills of interpretation, analysis and evaluation. There are many ways of preparing for an exam, but a thorough understanding of the material is obviously crucial.

Each chapter is structured to give a clear understanding of the authors, concepts and issues that you need to know about. To assist understanding and facilitate later revision it is often helpful to make short notes.

MAKING NOTES FROM THE BOOK

These should be short, relevant and complete.

- Include a page number so that you can locate the details again.
- Don't merely copy out sections; write them in your own words.
- They should be clear, so that they make sense when referred to again later.

You could try two systems to record points, which show how they are linked to an overall argument or theory. One can take the form of linear notes, and the other a pattern or diagram with arrows showing the way they relate together. A combination of both may be appropriate. Note-making, whether from a speaker, a video, audio tape or from a book, is a skill which requires practice. Devise a scheme which you use in a consistent way, using coloured pens.

Linear notes

- Bold headings establish key points: names, theories and concepts.
- Subheadings indicate details of relevant issues.
- A few numbered points list related arguments.

Diagrams

- Use a large blank sheet of paper and write a key idea in the centre.
- Make links between this and related issues.
- Show also the connections between sub issues which share features in common.

Both systems have their advantages and disadvantages, and may take some time to perfect. Linear notes can be little more than a copy of what is already in a book and patterned notes can be confusing. But if you practise the skill, they can reduce material efficiently and concisely, becoming invaluable for revision. Diagrammatic notes may be very useful for those with a strong visual memory and provide a clear overview of a whole issue, showing patterns of inter-connection. The introduction of helpful drawings or a touch of humour into the format is often a good way to facilitate the recall of names, research studies and complex concepts.

Study Points

- Produce effective evaluation notes by highlighting or underlining your text in different coloured pens; you could even use symbols or icons in the margins to depict strengths or weaknesses.
- Make a diagram to show the two ways of making notes with their possible advantages and disadvantages.

HOW TO FOCUS ON KEY ISSUES

Look for key authors, theories, concepts and issues, which are tabulated at the start of each chapter. The names of sociologists are important because they act as the hook on which you can hang related ideas, especially theories and research details. Their views may also be necessary with reference to coursework projects, or as sources for more detail. Definitions of terms and concepts are vital because you must become familiar with the language of sociology. There are excellent dictionaries of sociology available and it is important to have access to one. When reading in preparation for a written question, or to feel confident that you have covered the ground, it may be useful to:

- make summary diagrams which are legible and understandable for future reference

- decide on your interpretations of the points made. Do you tend to agree or disagree with the position they represent?
- discuss the ideas raised with someone else. Encourage them to ask you probing questions. This will reveal the extent of your understanding.
- decide where you stand in relation to questions about locality, community and nation; can you study the topic in a fairly detached way?

SKILLS ADVICE

Students must develop and display certain skills for their examination and recognise which ones are being tested in a question. The clues are frequently in key words in the opening part. The skill domains are:

1 **Knowledge and understanding**: the ability to discuss the views of the main theorists; their similarities and differences; the strengths and weaknesses of evidence. To gain marks students must display this when asked to *explain, examine, suggest a method, outline reasons.*
2 **Interpretation, application and analysis**: the use of evidence in a logical, relevant way, either to show how it supports arguments or refutes them. Students must show this ability when asked to *identify, use items A/B/C, draw conclusions from a table.*
3 **Evaluation**: the skill of assessing evidence in a balanced way so that logical conclusions follow. Students can recognise this skill when asked to *assess, critically examine, comment on levels of reliability, compare and contrast*; or if asked *to what extent.*

Study Points
Draw an evaluation table, as below, using the whole of an A4 page. Examine studies as you proceed in your work and fill in the relevant details. Keep it for revision purposes.

Sociologist		
Title of Study	Strengths	Weaknesses
Verdict		
Judgment/justification		

REVISION ADVICE

- Keep clear notes at all times in a file or on a disk (with back up copy).
- Be familiar with exam papers and their demands.
- Become familiar with key authors, their theories, their research and sociological concepts.

Activity
Make and keep **Key Concept Cards**, as shown below.

Collective Conscience

Key Idea

A term used by **Durkheim** meaning:

- The existence of a social and moral order exterior to individuals and acting upon them as an independent force.
- The shared sentiments, beliefs and values of individuals which make up the **collective conscience**.
- In **traditional societies** it forms the basis of social order.
- As societies modernise the collective conscience weakens: **mechanical solidarity** is replaced by **organic solidarity**.

Key theorist: Emile Durkheim

Syllabus area: Sociological Theories of Religion: Functionalism

EXAMINATION ADVICE

To develop an effective method of writing, answers should be:

- **Sociological**: use the language and research findings of sociologists; do not use anecdotal opinion gathered from people not involved in sociology to support arguments.
- **Adequate in length**: enough is written to obtain the marks available.
- **Interconnected** with other parts of the syllabus (such as stratification, gender, ethnicity).
- **Logical**: the answer follows from the relevant evidence.

- **Balanced**: arguments and counter arguments are weighed; references are suitable.
- **Accurate**: reliable data is obtained from many sources.

The **three skill** areas on p 3 should be **demonstrated** so that the question is answered effectively.

In displaying knowledge, the student is not necessarily also demonstrating interpretation.

- This must be specified with phrases like 'Therefore, this study leads to the view that ...'
- Sections of answers should hang together, one leading to the next. This shows how the question is being answered by a process of analysis based on the evidence.
- Reach a conclusion based on the evidence used and the interpretations made.

The skill of evaluation is often regarded (not necessarily accurately) as the most problematic. Evaluation means being judge and jury; the strengths and weaknesses of evidence is assessed and an overall judgment about its value is made. To evaluate an argument or theory, consider whether it usefully opens up debate; explains the events studied; does it have major weaknesses?

Activity

Look through some past examination papers and pick out the evaluation questions. Underline the evaluation words and work out which skills are required.

COURSEWORK ADVICE

Coursework provides an opportunity to carry out a study using primary and/or secondary data to investigate an issue of sociological interest. It must address theoretical issues and be based on one or more areas of the syllabus being studied. The suggestions included at the end of each chapter may be adapted or used to generate further ideas. This is where the discipline of sociology comes alive because here is an opportunity for you to gather your own information on localities and communities near you. But, before you begin, always take time to plan your intended research. Final decisions must be agreed with a teacher or tutor.

MAKING A PLAN

Before starting a piece of coursework, you should make a plan:

1 Read and make notes from articles describing research projects in journals.
2 Have a clear aim in mind; choose an issue that interests you and is within your ability.
3 Decide more precisely what you want to know; establish a simple hypothesis to test.
4 Select a range of possible methods; consider both quantitative and qualitative.
5 Decide on a range of possible sources of information.
6 List the people from whom you can seek help, perhaps including a statistician.

WRITING THE PROJECT

1 Seek frequent advice from a teacher or tutor.
2 Check the weighting for different objectives in the marking scheme.
3 Keep clear notes throughout, including new ideas and any problems that arise.
4 Limit its length (maximum 5,000 words).
5 Label and index the study in the following way:
   a **Rationale**: a reason for choosing the subject; preliminary observations on the chosen area
   b **Context**: an outline of the theoretical and empirical context of the study
   c **Methodology**: a statement of the methodology used and reasons for selecting it
   d **Content**: presentation of the evidence and/or argument including results
   e **Evaluation**: the outcomes are weighed and strengths and weaknesses noted
   f **Sources**: all the sources of information are listed.

2

THE DEVELOPMENT OF THE SOCIOLOGY OF LOCALITY, COMMUNITY AND NATION

Introduction

THIS CHAPTER WILL deal with the ways in which sociologists have developed the ideas of locality, community and nation since the nineteenth century. Its main concern is to explain the importance of the transition from a world that was mainly rural to one where towns and cities are the most common experience. We will outline why the rural-urban transition has been regarded as central to the discipline of the sociology. Together, these themes will be the focus throughout the first half of this book. How locality and community have been altered by the rise of nationalism and an awareness of national identity will be dealt with in the second half.

Table 1: *Theorists, Concepts and Issues in this chapter*		
KEY THEORISTS	KEY CONCEPTS	KEY ISSUES
Galpin, Kolb	Locality	What constitutes a locality?
Bell & Newby	Community	How is community defined?
Giddens	Nation	What is a nation?
Anderson	Imagined community	Why do we identify with people we will never meet?
Heller	Multiple identities	Which identities do we then choose?
Giddens	Postmodernity	Who are we? Where do we come from?
	Rural-urban continuum	How useful are sociological models?

Tönnies	*Gemeinschaft*	The rural or non-urban ideal type.
	Gesellschaft	The urban ideal type.
Bell & Newby	Class, status and power	Why are community studies criticised?
Cohen	Boundaries	How are boundaries formed?

This introductory chapter attempts to do three things:

- It begins with a discussion of the key concepts: locality, community, nation and identity.
- It traces the historiographical development of what is today called the sociology of locality, community and nation.
- It introduces the main themes which structure the text: competing and complementary identities. It is the concept of identity that links locality to community and to the nation.

THE CONCEPTS

'Locality', 'community', 'nation' and 'identity': these are some of the vaguest and most elusive of sociological concepts. They are also among the most important. The best way to unravel some of the confusion that surrounds them is look at how sociologists have used these terms and the meanings they have attached to them.

LOCALITY

Locality as a sociological concept has its roots in the work of the American rural sociologists Galpin (1920) and Kolb (1921). They defined a locality as the physical area in which economic and social life takes place. In their work they used the term 'locality group' to mean two things. Firstly, the locality group contains the important social institutions of a community. These include:

- Places of religious worship (churches, temples, mosques).
- Places of education and learning (schools, colleges, universities).
- Institutions dedicated to providing justice and maintaining law and order (legal offices, courts, police stations).

Secondly, in addition to containing the important social institutions of a community, the locality group also acts as a service centre. At a basic level, it is the place where people play their bingo in the church hall, do their shopping, pay their council tax, collect their pension or child benefit, and visit their dentist or doctor. The locality group may also offer a range of commercial leisure facilities (theatres, cinemas, swimming pools, squash courts) as well as museums, libraries and galleries.

COMMUNITY

The sociologists Colin Bell and Howard Newby (1971) have made the most important attempt to distinguish between the three distinct senses in which the word 'community' is used:

1 Community as topography – in this sense 'community' refers to the boundaries of a particular settlement.
2 Community as a local social system – this implies that there is a degree of social interconnection between local people and local institutions.
3 Community as 'communion' – used in this way 'community' evokes images of a common bond, warmth of feeling between people and a sense of belonging. *Belonging*, for example, is the title of a famous collection of studies of small rural communities, edited by the anthropologist Anthony P. Cohen (1982).

Study Point
Before reading the next section, write down three things that you associate with the word 'nation'.

NATION

The sense of belonging is an essential component of the nation and of national identity. Loyalty to the nation or the nation-state has been probably the most powerful, and perhaps even the most destructive, force of the nineteenth and twentieth centuries. A nation can be defined as 'a collectivity existing within a clearly demarcated territory' while a nation-state 'exists within a complex of other nation-states' and where a state governs 'a territory with demarcated boundaries (borders)' (Giddens 1985).

Yet for the nation and the nation-state to engender loyalty to it, for its people to express their nationality, there is formed a wider sense of the 'national' community. This can be understood in the well-known phrase of Benedict Anderson, the 'imagined community' (1991). Its significance is in explaining how we can claim common cause and common attachment to people we have never met and never will meet.

THE MANY FACES OF IDENTITY

Locality, community and nation are the three spheres in which social life occurs. It is important to realise that these spheres are not isolated and independent of each other but are interrelated and interdependent. Individuals are social actors who create localities, communities and nations simultaneously. We relate to these by and through the concept of identity.

The concept of identity is an extremely complex one. This is partly because identity is a term which is used in a very wide sense and appears to apply to anything of a national, local, cultural or religious nature. Sometimes these all seem to merge together, as in the case of the Welsh woman who lives in Leominster, is a Methodist, supports Liverpool Football Club, and waved her Union Jack when the Queen Mother opened a war memorial. Here are seven different identities at least!

To consider a Scottish example, it is often said that a person from any of the towns in the Scottish Borders is conscious of having three identities and indeed prides themselves on this fact. At one and the same time they are a citizen of their particular town, for example, Hawick, Galashiels, Melrose, or Peebles; a Borderer; and a Scot. These different identities blend into one another and become fused during local festivals such as the annual Common Ridings, and international rugby matches when players from the various Border teams frequently make up the Scottish national team.

From these examples it seems as if identities are both something we are born with and something we can choose (or not choose) to acquire. There is also a sense in which they can be called up, for example, during moments of crisis, and dismissed at will. Identity is an extremely elusive concept!

The Hungarian philosopher Agnes Heller (1984) offers a useful way of understanding this most slippery of sociological concepts. Heller argues that identity is about both what we are at birth and what we choose to become. Certain identities are fixed for they are there when we are born. A person cannot alter the fact that they have been born into a particular family, in a particular locality, community and nation. Heller calls these facets of identity 'particularistic'. At the same time, she argues, there is a sense in which identity is not fixed but is 'individualistic'. As the person grows up they begin to select from the range of identities provided by the social environment. They may, for example, choose to support Liverpool Football Club, to vote for the Labour Party, to become a vegetarian, to join the National Trust, to become a New Age Traveller, or to assert their national identity by writing Scottish, Welsh, Northern Irish or English on official forms.

Study Point

Suggest three areas of day-to-day life that give you the strongest feelings of an identity. Explain why they are significant.

POST MODERNITY AND LOCALITY, COMMUNITY AND NATION

At this point it is important to consider the concept of postmodernity and its relevance to the sociology of locality, community and nation. At a basic level, the argument behind postmodernity is that a new social order is in the process of emerging. The precise form that this new society will take is unclear but is very different from anything that has gone before. In this new society nothing can be known with certainty because all pre-existing foundations of knowledge have been shown to be unreliable. There is talk of the 'end of history' because past, present, and the future seem to merge. New social movements appear and foreshadow the arrival of a social and political order (Giddens 1990).

The arguments surrounding postmodernity are extremely complex and we will not enter into this debate in any great detail. Its relevance to the sociology of locality, community and nation lies in the fact that postmodernity has introduced the possibility of multiple identities into the arena of everyday life. It has raised questions of 'who are we?', 'where do we come from?', and 'where are we going?' and given them a greater political significance than ever before.

POINTS OF EVALUATION

Three key points emerge from this introductory discussion and will be repeated throughout this book:

1 Individuals create localities, communities and nations simultaneously and relate to these through and by the concept of identity.
2 Individuals have multiple identities which are sometimes competing and sometimes conflicting.
3 Certain identities are there at birth but others are acquired throughout life.

Activity
Make a list of the key features of your locality, your community and your nation. Inevitably there will be much overlap in your choices, but try to find six indicators of each concept as we have defined them so far.

THE DEVELOPMENT OF THE SOCIOLOGY OF LOCALITY, COMMUNITY AND NATION

The origins of the sociology of locality, community and nation can be traced back to the nineteenth century when early sociologists were attempting to make sense of the great changes brought about by the Industrial Revolution and the French Revolution which had begun a century earlier (Nisbet 1967). In their efforts to understand what was going on all around them they constructed a series of 'models' against which reality could be tested. The 'rural-urban' continuum is one of these models and it lies at the heart of the sociology of locality, community, and nation.

It is important to realise that the rural–urban continuum does not provide a complete or comprehensive description of either the rural or the urban sectors of any society. Rather, it is best thought of as a line running between two poles. The 'rural' pole stands for small, inward-looking, idyllic communities whose economy is mainly based on agriculture and whose primary relationships are essentially formed around an extended family. By contrast the 'urban' pole represents large, impersonal, cosmopolitan, industrial and commercial centres.

Table 2 outlines the historical development of the rural–urban continuum.

Table 2: *Contributors to the development of the rural–urban continuum*		
AUTHOR	RURAL OR NON-URBAN	URBAN
Sir Henry Maine (1861)	Status	Contract
Hebert Spencer (1862)	Military	Industrial
Ferdinand Tönnies (1887)	*Gemeinschaft*	*Gesellschaft*
Emile Durkheim (1893)	Mechanical solidarity	Organic solidarity
Max Weber (1922)	Traditional	Rational
Robert Redfield (1947)	Folk	Urban
Howard Becker (1950)	Sacred	Secular

(SOURCE: JONES (1973), AFTER REISSMAN (1964))

The contributions of Maine, Spencer, Durkheim, Weber, Redfield and Becker to the construction of the rural-urban continuum are all important. We will encounter their influence throughout the ideas discussed in this book. The work of the nineteenth–century German sociologist, Ferdinand Tönnies has, however, had most impact on the development of the sociology of locality, community and nation. We will look at his work in some detail, then show how his key ideas have been modified and altered.

DISTINCTIONS BETWEEN *GEMEINSCHAFT* AND *GESELLSCHAFT*

Tönnies identified two contrasting ways of living: *Gemeinschaft* and *Gesellschaft*. Loosely translated, *Gemeinschaft* means community in the sense of 'communion'. It closely resembles the notion of a big family – of blood ties (where you are always part of your family even once you have left home). *Gesellschaft*, however, in the words of Elias (1974), represents a colder, unattached and more fragmented way of living devoid of cooperation and social cohesion. Instead of a sense of neighbourliness, people are isolated. *Gesellschaft* translates as association. You pay your money and you take your choice – associations are there for you to join (by paying your membership) and to leave. There are no blood commitments. Others have called this 'civil society'. *Gesellschaft* is much more impersonal and is more characteristic of urban life than it is of the hamlet, the village or the crofting township.

Major Characteristics of Gemeinschaft *and* Gesellschaft

It is important to realise that the concepts of *Gemeinschaft* and *Gesellschaft* are ideal types – they consist of all the characteristic elements of the social feature being analysed. The ideal type is never true of the real world, but its use gives a means of exploring these variations and differences. Table 3 lists the major characteristics of *Gemeinschaft* and *Gesellschaft* in their ideal typical form.

Table 3: *The ideal types of* Gemeinschaft *and* Gesellschaft: *social characteristics*		
SOCIAL CHARACTERISTICS	GEMEINSCHAFT	GESELLSCHAFT
Dominant social relationships	Kinship, locality and neighbourliness, fellowship – 'Common goods – common evils; common friends – common enemies'.	Exchange, rational calculation specific function … 'everybody is by himself and isolated, and there exists a condition of tension against all others'.
Ordering of social institutions	Family life, rural village life, town life.	City life, national life, cosmopolitan life.
Characteristic form of wealth	Land	Money
Central institution and forms of social control	Family law, extended kinship, group, concord, customs and mores, religion.	The state, convention, contracts, political legislation, public opinion.
Status-role	Everyone's role fully integrated in the system, the status of each being ascribed.	Role based on each specific relationship, the status in each being based on personal achievement.

(SOURCE: DERIVED FROM JONES, 1973)

Points of Evaluation

1 Tönnies believed that *Gemeinschaft* and *Gesellschaft* were stages of historical development.

2 He was well aware that at the time he was writing he was living through the transformation of *Gemeinschaft* into *Gesellschaft*. He was not entirely happy with this. Consequently, *Gemeinschaft* became a cherished ideal, a world to which he would like to return.

3 *Gemeinschaft* has also become associated with images of the rural idyll which are prevalent in the sociology of locality and community in the 1990s. These issues will be discussed in detail in Chapter 3.

Study Points

- Suggest five reasons why people living 100 years ago would be more likely to have stronger feelings of *Gemeinschaft* than those living today.

- In which areas of the country would feelings of *Gesellschaft* be strongest?

THE EMERGENCE OF INTEREST IN URBAN INDUSTRIAL SOCIETY

The founding fathers of sociology (Emile Durkheim, Karl Marx and Max Weber) paid little attention to rural life. The dominant concerns of these three men were focused instead on urban areas. They considered rural areas to be archaic and backward looking, while urban areas were modern and progressive. They believed that the profound economic and social changes which were taking place in the towns and cities (the process of industrialisation) would gradually modernise rural life. It was a question of time.

Indeed, until the 1940s British sociology as a discipline remained essentially urban and industrial in outlook. Then, following the end of the Second World War and the major restructuring problems the conflict had created, the issue of food security became increasingly important. Political attention became focused on rural areas in general and the strategic role of the agricultural sector in particular. Farmers were encouraged to produce as much food as possible in order to make Britain self-sufficient in the event of future conflict. Yet the primary aim of agricultural work was theorised only in terms of sustaining the towns and cities. Mainstream British sociology, from the end of the Second World War and up until the late 1960s, was seen largely as a science, the aim of which was to understand and resolve social problems. These social problems, it was believed, originated and existed primarily in Britain's towns and cities and were related to housing, health and education. As a result the outlook of postwar British sociology remained urban and industrial rather than rural and agricultural.

THE DEVELOPMENT OF THE 'COMMUNITY STUDIES' SCHOOL OF THOUGHT

While most sociologists concerned themselves with the problems of urban, industrial Britain, a minority of researchers focused their attention on rural localities. Between the 1940s and 1960s these intrepid researchers carried out 'community studies'. Some of the most important are W.M. Williams: *The Sociology of an English Village: Gosforth* (1964); Ronald Frankenberg: *Village on the Border* (1957); James Littlejohn's study *Westrigg* in the Scottish Borders (1963), and, for the city, two contributions by Michael Young and Peter Willmott to a series of publications by the Institute of Community Studies: *Family and Kinship in East London* (1957) and *Family and Class in a London Suburb* (1960).

Apart from being a particularly good example of a community study, Frankenberg's *Village on the Border* provides some valuable insights into the relationship between locality, community and nation. *Village on the Border* is a study of the political life of the village of Pentrediwaith in North Wales, near the English Border, focusing on the activities of the parish council and the issues of education and employment. It shows how these problems are affected by class allegiances, religious affiliations, and by the place of the community and the locality in the nation.

Activity

Compare the evidence used to indicate a 'community' in the studies mentioned. Try to identify the key point which underlies the researcher's analysis from the three extracts shown below. Once you have made your list, write 50 words on the strength of the community study as an approach to sociological research.

The village of Gosforth is unusually large for this area of West Cumberland. ... The area generally has ... clung to its traditional diffused social life which links up the scattered farms. Even in Gosforth the farmers tend to depend upon one another for fellowship, and this self-contained life of the countryside has impeded the development of the village as a social centre. ... Urban centres have few attractions for the countryfolk, and apart from a small number who go to Whitehaven once a week on market day, visits to the town are confined to 'special occasions'.

(Williams, 1964)

'They're all the same these peddlers, they just think we country people don't know what the right prices are.' Shortly after this I learned from one of the housewife's relatives that she (the housewife) had bought over two pounds worth of goods from the peddler. In other words, all the time she had been speaking to me she had simply been trying to destroy a conception of herself which she feared I (a townsman) might have of her – a conception of herself as one ignorant of the right price of linen goods, a country person.

(Littlejohn, 1963)

The mother is naturally more likely to know about people moving out, or planning to move out, in her own particular part of Bethnal Green. This is one reason why daughters get accommodation near her. Not only is her knowledge more complete, her influence with landlords and rent collectors is also greater. She knows personally the man collecting the rent, who often does so for several other nearby houses, and very often it is he who in effect selects tenants for any premises that become unoccupied.

… 'My mother has lived here for years and my sisters were all living here. We knew the collector and spoke to him. That's how we got this place'.

(Young and Willmott, 1957)

Points of Evaluation

1 Community studies were popular during the 1940s, 1950s, and 1960s. They relied very heavily on anthropological/ethnographic approaches.

2 They were highly detailed, microcosmic studies of social life in one geographically small area.

3 They shared a common theme of communities in transition. Most of the communities studied were experiencing profound social changes and this was resulting in the loss of the traditional social order. In other words, they were snapshots of the movement from *Gemeinschaft* to *Gesellschaft*.

4 By the 1970s community studies were being criticised for relying on description rather than analysis; for being non-quantitative and too reliant upon subjective and impressionistic data. They were cameos of social life in places that were often physically, geographically and socially distinct. Consequently, it was hard to make any valid generalisations on the basis of research carried out in these areas.

5 The most important criticisms of community studies came from the sociologists Colin Bell and Howard Newby whose pioneering work highlighted the limitations of community studies and offered an exciting new way of studying rural areas. What Bell and Newby did was to break away from the anthropological/ethnographic approach used and to apply in a systematic fashion fundamental sociological concepts such as class, status and power to the study of social life in rural areas.

6 Bell and Newby's study of East Anglican farmers and farm workers (written with colleagues Saunders and Rose, 1978) gave an account of the third quarter of the twentieth century in which the historic constraints on farmers were removed, and in which, following the postwar settlement, they came to dominate food production in the UK. Apart from showing how farmers were powerful in market, work and status situations, Bell and Newby helped to shape the future agenda for sociological research on rural areas.

Suggest three reasons why it is hard to make generalisations from a descriptive study of a working class area in the 1950s.

THE EMERGENCE OF A MULTI-DISCIPLINARY APPROACH

Another important milestone in the development of the sociology of locality, community and nation was the foundation of the Rural Economy & Society Study Group (RESSG) in 1979. The aim of the RESSG was to provide a forum for all those studying the social formation of rural areas in advanced societies. From the start the RESSG was multi-disciplinary in outlook, combining the work of sociologists, geographers, agricultural economists and political scientists. As such it was indicative of the new agenda for studying the sociology of the rural world.

Deprivation

Since the 1980s the sociology of locality, community and nation has become increasingly multi-disciplinary and policy-orientated. It has become less theoretical and more practical in outlook, focusing on social problems such as the related issues of deprivation and disadvantage.

'Deprivation' is generally thought of an imbalance between needs and resources:

Deprivation ... has no precise meaning, but a household can be said to be deprived when its welfare falls beyond some generally agreed standards. The concept goes beyond the single notion of financial poverty, i.e., insufficient income in terms of some standard of need, to encompass other aspects of welfare observed former influenced by the activities of the state, for example, the provision of health care, education, housing, and recreational provision.

(Miller, 1980)

'Disadvantage' is in many ways similar to 'deprivation' but goes one step further by emphasising that individuals and households are not to blame:

'Disadvantage' in the sense used in this report refers to the inability of individuals or households to share in styles of life open to the majority. It does not imply any failing on their own part. This is very close to the concept of social exclusion, developed during EU discussions of poverty and disadvantage, which emphasises the forces of social and economic restructuring and the exercise of systematic power in society in disadvantaging or excluding people.

(Shucksmith et al, 1994)

Deprivation and disadvantage are generally thought of as problems occurring in small pockets in urban areas. Government policies to combat deprivation have been designed with this assumption in mind. Little attention has been paid to rural areas, yet deprivation and disadvantage can also be found lurking behind the rural idyll.

Study Points

- Suggest three reasons why little attention has been paid to deprivation in rural areas.
- In what ways is deprivation likely to be severe, yet disguised?

In 1985 Mclaughlin carried out a study of rural poverty in England. He looked at five case study areas and suggested that 25 per cent of rural households were living in poverty or were on the margins of poverty.

A decade later Midwinter and Monaghan attempted to measure and analyse the extent of rural deprivation in Scotland by studying five areas. They found that not only is rural deprivation extensive in Scotland but it takes a number of forms. They point to a clear pattern of service under-provision and a high cost of living. These problems are reinforced and compounded by a poor public transport system.

In their research into disadvantage among elderly people in north Ayrshire, Angus, Wester Ross, and the Island of Harris, Shucksmith and colleagues (1994) made the important point that deprivation and disadvantage are not ghettoised, as they tend to be in urban areas, but dispersed. This means that it is not so easy to develop a coordinated and specific strategy to help rural communities.

The problems associated with rural deprivation and disadvantage are beginning to be recognised as the following quotation from the Newsletter of the Community Council in Shropshire (August 1995) makes clear:

POVERTY IN SHROPSHIRE?

One might at first not associate the county of Shropshire as being faced with severe problems relating to poverty. In comparison with the third world both Shropshire and the UK are relatively well off. However, in the UK it is mainly the urban conurbations which are associated with poverty and deprivation. The recognition of rural areas suffering from problems has begun to be accepted. The establishment of the Shropshire Rural Development Area and the Marches Objective 5b area are testimony to that. However, amongst the general public Shropshire is still seen as a beautiful county. Well of course it is, but hidden behind the magnificent countryside is a situation in stark contrast.

- Average wages – third lowest in the country
- a lack of affordable housing
- lack of public transport system to serve the needs of local people
- implications of delivering community care to an increasingly elderly population, and a lack of job opportunities in the countryside.

Activity

Using the terms *Gemeinschaft* and *Gesellschaft* as your headings, evaluate the pros and cons of the 'community study' approach in making sense of life in the village and life in the town today. Conclude on the challenge of 'deprivation' to the coherence of the 'community'.

THE LOCALITY AND THE COMMUNITY

We have mentioned the social anthropologist Anthony P. Cohen and his work on boundaries. He has also written about the island of Whalsay in the Shetland Isles. In this study he tries to understand the link between locality and community by showing how boundaries are formed:

> 'Community' suggests that its putative members have something in common with each other which distinguishes them in a significant manner from the members of other groups. The term thus seems to imply simultaneously the opposition of the community to others or to other social entities ...
>
> The boundary is thus more complex than its physical, legal or administrative bases; more complex than the ethnic, racial, religious or linguistic differences which it may enclose. Many of the elements which constitute the boundary may not be objectively apparent at all but, rather, exist in the minds of their beholders. Like other symbols, the boundary does not entail given meanings. Rather, it provides people with forms which they may then invest with meaning ...
>
> *(Cohen 1987)*

There are a number of important points which arise from this text, and we have summarised them in the diagram below:

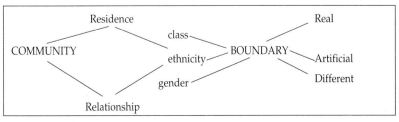

A community is characterised by a delimited area of residence, with either a stable or fluid population, who perceive themselves in complex relationships and different from others (other communities). This sense of community is strong enough to override potential conflicts over class, ethnicity or gender. This achieves a sense of boundary between 'us' and 'them'; a boundary that may be physical (such as a wall), but is usually an artificial construct (imaginary). The boundary is perceived differently by different members of the community, yet all still regard it as significant.

Activity

Think about the way that boundaries are constructed around communities. Take where you live as your example and try to establish how it creates boundaries between itself and other communities nearby. If you have time, you could devise a set of questions you would like to ask of your neighbours, community leaders, or friends in any social group. These questions should concentrate on how 'us' and 'them' are constructed. Write up your conclusion in 300–500 words.

SUMMARY

Chapter 2 has introduced the key concepts of locality, community, nation and identity. It has made the important points that locality, community and nation are the three spheres in which social life occurs. These spheres are not isolated and independent of each other but are interrelated and interdependent. Individuals relate to locality, community and nation by and through the concept of identity.

The ideas of locality, community and nation have been developed since the nineteenth century by sociologists seeking to explain the importance of the transition from a world which was mainly rural to one where towns and cities are the most common experience. The rural–urban continuum is the product of this intellectual endeavour. It is central to understanding how the sociology of locality, community and nation has changed and what it attempts to do.

Group work

Divide the class into three separate groups, each concentrating on one aspect of this topic:

What is a locality, what is community, what is a nation?

1 Members of Group 1 to draw a map of their locality; members of group 2 to draw a map of their community; members of group 3 to draw a map of their nation.

2 In each case, mark its boundaries, and justify the drawing up of boundaries to the locality, community or nation. To the maps each group should add a list of its main features, such as its buildings, housing, people, ethnic composition, cultural markers, defining symbols. One member of each group to discuss their maps and lists with the class as a whole.

3 Consider the differences and similarities which arise for people as to the nature and extent of their conceptions of these areas. Extract the differences and similarities between locality, community and nation. Illustrate the problems for doing sociological research on these perceptions.

Coursework

1 'A community study of a village near a large urban centre'
Focus on a small village, and create a questionnaire to concentrate on the interaction between neighbours and their families. The power of the community study lies in the depth of data it can unearth linked to everyday experiences. To what extent is there a 'community' present?

2 'A study of class, status and power in a rural setting'
Your aim here is to provide a critique of the community study approach by taking the much broader sociological concepts of class, status and power as your analytical tools. A questionnaire would be a good approach. Concentrate on unequal relationships and the types of social interaction that occur amongst a dense network of family, friends and neighbours.

Exam hints

When reading this chapter and those that follow, always try to ask yourself two questions. First, 'What key points am I being asked to learn?'. Secondly, 'What are the ways in which an examiner, having read this book, could ask questions about it?'. A specimen examination question is given below:

'*Because the concept of 'community' is defined in so many different ways, it is of little use to an understanding of rural and urban life in modern society.' Critically discuss this statement with reference to relevant sociological studies.*

This question can be answered from the empirical and theoretical information provided in this chapter but you will not be able to produce a complete answer until you have read the remaining chapters in this book (particularly Chapters 3–5).

Revision hints

From this chapter, you should now understand the following themes. Take time to make a key concept card on each:

- A definition of locality, community and nation.
- The meaning of identity.
- The rural–urban continuum.
- *Gemeinschaft* and *Gesellschaft*.
- The community study.
- A critique of the community study.
- A multi-disciplinary approach to understanding the community.
- How boundaries are constructed and maintained.

Practice questions

1 What attempts have been made to establish a rural–urban continuum by sociologists? Critically discuss two examples.
2 Distinguish between the concepts of locality and community. Illustrate, with reference to studies, the ways in which their significance and relevance has been analysed by sociologists.

3

CHANGE IN THE COUNTRYSIDE

Introduction

THE AIM OF this chapter is to explore the reality of *Gemeinschaft* – just what changes have occurred in the countryside, the rural world. This reality is often ignored because the ideological power of *Gemeinschaft* lies in its promotion of an ideal way of life. We are not dealing with something that is false or mistaken, but its influence in our interpretation of locality, community and nation is an idealised one. We shall discuss the 'rural idyll' as the most explicit way that the concept of *Gemeinschaft* exerts its ideological power. But we shall also consider the important structural changes that have taken place in the countryside because these reflect modern society just as our towns and cities do. The rural and the urban are at opposite ends of a continuum, as we argued in Chapter 2, and this means their relationship with each other is always active. We cannot understand the growth and dominance of urban life without understanding the changes that have taken place in the countryside in the modern period.

Table 4: *Theorists, concepts and issues in this chapter*		
KEY THEORISTS	KEY CONCEPTS	KEY ISSUES
Williams	Rural idyll	Was there a golden age?
The Scott Report	Postwar rural policy	Promoting agriculture and the town
Yearley	Environmentalism	Agricultural productivity v ecological preservation
Morris & Gladstone	Farm tourism	How have farmers diversified?
MacNee	Commuters, good lifers	Why do people leave cities?

Newby	Country stereotypes	Why 'conflicting ideals' of the countryside?
McCrone, Morris, Kiely	Heritage and conservation	Why do people join heritage and conservation societies?
McCrone	The 'land' as ideology	How does 'land' create community? How does 'land' create national identity?

THE RURAL IDYLL

Statistics may readily and coldly prove the population of England to be by majority urban rather than rural; industrial rather than agricultural; yet we shall submit without much fear of contradiction that some peculiar and essential virtue of the English character sucks up its life from the roots buried in that baffling, contradictory, yet unwavering product of centuries, the countryman. He was here long before the industrial worker was here, and is thus not only the immediate grandfather but also the remote ancestor of our mechanically minded young men. Such pressure of heredity, so continuous a strain, cannot be ignored: its hidden thread in our tapestry is too strong.

V. Sackville-West, 'Outdoor Life' in E. Barker (ed) *The Character of England* (1947) Oxford

During the nineteenth century the population of Britain increased dramatically, from 10.5 million in 1801 to 33 million in 1891. This was accompanied by an equally dramatic shift in the distribution of the population as people left the rural areas and moved in search of new occupations to the emerging towns and cities. By the middle of the nineteenth century the majority of the British population lived, for the first time, in urban settlements with populations over 2500.

This exodus of the British population from the countryside and the corresponding growth of urban areas was captured in the literature and art of the period. Just as Tönnies' concept of *Gemeinschaft* became a cherished ideal of a world to which he would like to return, novelists, poets, and painters reflected the great changes going on all around them and mourned the passing of an idealised rural way of life (see Mingay 1989). What is often referred to as the 'rural idyll' is important because it provides the key to how we think about the countryside today. It is only by acknowledging the importance of art and literature in influencing the way we think about the countryside that we can begin to understand the wider process of rural change.

LITERATURE

In his important work *The Country and the City* (1973), Raymond Williams made the point that throughout English literature we are constantly referred back to successive 'golden ages', of a rural 'Old England' which is located firmly in the childhood of the authors and about to vanish. The poems by the herd-boy and farmer, John Clare, written in the early nineteenth century about his native Northamptonshire are a lament for a countryside which is about to vanish. Thomas Hardy's novels and poems which were written later in the century but set in the 1820s and 1830s, continue this theme.

ART

Nostalgic urban patrons were eager to buy paintings depicting a pastoral idea which they believed was being threatened by rapid and large-scale industrial development. It is there in the paintings of the group of artists who, in 1848, formed themselves into the Pre-Raphaelite Brotherhood. Inspired by the search for truth in the representation of nature, Pre-Raphaelite paintings are rich in moral and religious symbolism. Many Pre-Raphaelite paintings depict a quiet countryside scene in late summer or autumn. Ford Madox Brown's *An English Autumn Afternoon*, and *Pretty Baa Lambs* are good examples of the genre.

The Pre-Raphaelite Brotherhood disbanded in the mid-1850s but nature continued to be an important subject for Victorian art. The paintings of Myles Birket Foster (1825–99) and Helen Allingham portrayed scenes of sentimental, rosy-cheeked rusticity, of quaint country cottages, and children playing. Although poor in appearance, the children in these pictures were always happy. These sanitised and idealised pictures of rural life appealed to the Victorians and were in stark contrast to the horrors of urban life which were all around them. They were also images of the countryside which have become deeply embedded in modern consciousness and form the basis of the rural idyll.

Study Point

Explain the concept of 'rural idyll'. Is it one you share?

CHANGE IN THE COUNTRYSIDE

Since 1900 the British countryside has changed considerably in terms of:

- its physical appearance;
- what the land is used for;
- its social composition;
- how it is perceived by those who live there, leading to conflicting ideals of rural life.

CHANGES IN THE PHYSICAL APPEARANCE OF THE COUNTRYSIDE

While some of the remote parts of upland Britain, for example, North West Sutherland in Scotland, have changed little in terms of physical appearance, other parts of the British countryside look very different today from how they did even 30 years ago. In some places the changes have been gradual and subtle, for example, a piece of rough pasture may have been drained, fenced, ploughed, and re-seeded, or a dirt track may have been replaced by a proper road. Other changes have been more dramatic.

WENLOCK EDGE, SHROPSHIRE

A MODERN HOUSING ESTATE

This is the land of lost content,
I see it shining plain
The happy highways where I went
And cannot come again.
(Housman 1939)

Other examples of dramatic changes in the visual appearance of the countryside, include:

- A motorway built through a valley.
- A copse where snowdrops, primroses, and bluebells once grew being cleared to make way for wheat.
- The planting of fast growing, improved conifers (Sitka Spruce, Lodge Pine, Norway Spruce, and Douglas Fir) in many parts of rural Scotland immediately after the Second World War (and up until the late 1980s when tax breaks were removed) as part of the drive to increase timber production. There has been a tendency for vast tracts of land to be planted with a single species, providing blanket-like cover on the hills. Many of these conifers are now coming up to felling age and the land is being replanted with a greater variety of species. In another 30 years the landscape could once again look very different.

These changes in the physical appearance of the British countryside are a direct result of changes in what land is used for.

THE CHANGING LAND-USE STRUCTURE OF THE BRITISH COUNTRYSIDE

The British countryside is a managed countryside. In October 1941, under the chairmanship of Lord Justice Scott, the official Committee on Land Utilisation in Rural Areas laid out the philosophy and objectives which have guided rural policy since the Second World War. The Scott Report was based on the belief that a prosperous farming industry would preserve both the rural landscape and rural communities.

The assumptions contained within the Scott Report were embedded in the Agriculture Act 1947, the Town and Country Planning Act 1947 and the National Parks and Access to the Countryside Act 1949. Between them these three acts established a postwar policy framework for rural areas. This is well discussed in Rogers (1989) and Allanson and Whitby (1996):

- The main concern of the Agriculture Act 1947 was food and timber production. It sought to maintain the predominance of agriculture in the countryside.
- The aim of the Town & Country Planning Act 1947 was urban containment. It sought to protect agricultural land from urban encroachment.
- The National Parks and Access to the Countryside Act 1949 was inspired by a vision of the countryside as the heritage of the whole nation. It sought to ensure both landscape and nature conservation, and recreational access. It established the National Parks Commission (England & Wales). Under the 1949 Act local authorities became involved in protecting areas of outstanding natural beauty and encouraging greater access to the countryside via established rights of way.

The postwar public policy framework for rural areas was, therefore, dominated by the issues of food and timber production; urban containment; conservation and access to the countryside. There have been high levels of state intervention and planning to ensure that these objectives are met.

Points of Evaluation

1 State intervention has taken two forms: through economic support for agriculture, or through town and country planning.
2 State intervention and planning have affected the uses to which both agricultural and non-agricultural land is put.
3 Responsibility for agricultural land has been lodged with economic planners in the Ministry of Agriculture. They have encouraged agricultural production by offering subsidies to farmers.
4 Non-agricultural land has been the responsibility of town and country planners working in local authority planning departments. They have sought to protect the countryside from the ills of excessive urban encroachment.

Activity
Discuss the changes which have occurred in land use in the area in which you live or study with someone who has seen the changes occur over time. Have they all been well received or subject to criticism? Do the critics or those who favour the changes share any features in common, such as age, gender or class?

Agricultural support and planning

The origins of planned support for agriculture can be traced back to the 1920s and 1930s when British farming was in severe depression. The Wheat Act of 1932 was the first measure of planned support for British agriculture.

Planned support for agriculture increased immediately after the end of the Second World War. The year 1946 saw the creation of the National Agricultural Advisory Services (NAAS). This became the Agricultural Development & Advisory Service (ADAS). This was a prelude to the 1947 Agriculture Act. The 1947 Act is extremely important. It marked the beginning of a close relationship between the government and farmers through their union, the National Farmers Union/Scottish Farmers Union (NFU)/(SFU).

In 1973 Britain joined the European Economic Community (EEC), now called the European Community (EC or, increasingly, the European Union (EU)). Entry to the EEC meant that decisions affecting farmers would now come from Brussels as well as from Whitehall.

National land-use planning

Similarly, the origins of national land-use planning can be traced back to the depression of the 1920s and 1930s, culminating in the Town & Country Planning Act 1947 and the National Parks & Access to the Countryside Act 1949.

The aim of the latter Act was to ensure landscape and nature conservation and recreational access to the countryside. This it did quite successfully until the 1960s when a worldwide tourism boom occurred. Tourism to remote and rural areas became increasingly popular. This caused important questions to be raised about the uses to which land is put and how land should be managed. The result was the passing of the Countryside Act in 1968 which transformed the National Parks Commission into the Countryside Commission (CC). As its name suggests, the CC is responsible for landscape protection and recreation provision not just within the National Parks, but throughout the countryside.

Study Point
Suggest reasons why the depression of the 1920s and 1930s gave rise to the development of legislation to land use.

Tourism and the environment: the balance sheet

From the 1970s onwards the debate, in policy-making circles, about tourism as a form of land use has taken place against a backcloth of growing environmental awareness. 'Green' activists were becoming increasingly concerned about such issues as: the 'hole' in the ozone layer; global warming; the loss of habitats and species evolution; threats to food and water; waste and waste disposal; exhaust fumes from vehicles and acid rain (Yearley 1991).

By the late 1980s environmental awareness had become such an important political and social issue that it featured prominently in all debates about tourism as a form of land use. Many of these debates have hinged on the issue of tourism as a form of sustainable rural development. Tourism and the environment are seen as a kind of balance sheet. The tourism industry is very dependent on the quality of the environment. Visitors are attracted to clean, green, litter-free places precisely because they are clean, green and litter-free. They can easily become spoiled by mountain bikes, litter from picnics, campsites and purpose-built holiday home developments. If these things happen, then the very qualities which attracted visitors to the area in the first place, will have been destroyed.

Farm tourism: an example of sustainable tourism

Since the mid-1980s there has been a major restructuring of the EC agricultural support system to take greater account of market forces. The UK ALURE package of 1987 and the Farm Diversification Grant Scheme of the following year were introduced to encourage farmers to diversify out of agriculture. The effects of these policy measures were compounded by the MacSharry reforms of the Common Agricultural Policy (CAP) in 1992 which made arable farmers take land out of production and altered the support structure for cereals.

An important result of these changes in the agricultural support system has been to make tourism increasingly attractive to farmers and their families. The development of tourism on farms has proved popular both with farmers and with policy-makers because it offers a way of combining support for the economy of rural areas with custodianship of agricultural land.

In addition to regenerating the rural economy and caring for the countryside, farm tourism has opened up new opportunities for women on farms. The most important of these include providing a source of additional income and helping to ease the loneliness that can sometimes accompany living on a remote or isolated farm. In their study of farm tourism in the Orkney Islands, Perthshire, and South Ayrshire, Morris and Gladstone (1997) found that in each case it was the farmer's wife who was responsible for the management of the farm tourism enterprise. Most of the women interviewed stressed that while they welcomed the extra income, they also did it because they enjoyed doing it and liked meeting interesting people. One respondent in the Orkney Islands went as far as to say that she did bed and breakfast simply because she loved the sociability it brought. She was not sure how much, if any, profit she actually made!

Study Point
Suggest how a piece of research could be undertaken in your locality to study the significance of tourism for women.

THE CHANGING SOCIAL COMPOSITION OF THE BRITISH COUNTRYSIDE

At the outbreak of the Second World War less than one person in five lived in the countryside. By the beginning of the 1960s things were beginning to change. The major urban centres, especially the big conurbations, started to lose population while the population of rural areas began to increase. Between 1961 and 1971 Greater London lost 6.8 per cent of its population, and between 1971 and 1981 lost a further 10.1 per cent. The pattern has been much the same in other metropolitan districts.

The gaps in British cities created by so many people moving to rural areas are being filled by immigrants. A third of all immigrants into Britain settle in Greater London. Ethnic minorities tend to live in the less affluent neighbourhoods of towns and cities. More than 60 per cent of Pakistani and Bangladeshi immigrants live on council estates or in poor areas (*The Times*, 30 January 1997). The relationship between race and housing will be explored in detail in Chapter 4.

The population of rural areas, from the remote, less accessible districts, to small towns and villages, increased by 17 per cent between 1971 and 1995. This movement of people from the large towns and cities into the countryside is known as the process of counter-urbanisation and is one of the major themes of Chapter 5.

Two obvious results of the process of counter-urbanisation are more populous villages and small towns. A less obvious, but arguably more important, result concerns the fact that the new inhabitants of the countryside are urban people who bring with them different attitudes, values, aspirations, and ideals. The new rural dwellers include:

Commuters

From the 1930s onwards the railway system and the new arterial roads made it possible to live in the country and work in the towns and cities. The development of a motorway network and a speedier intercity train service after the Second World War made commuting easier than it had ever been before.

A study of living in rural Scotland carried out by Karen MacNee in 1996 found that 31 per cent of all employed adults living in the small villages outside the town of Stirling were commuters. Most of these (25 per cent) travelled to work in Stirling itself and the remaining 11 per cent to Glasgow. This group have used their purchasing power in the housing market to buy in to the 'rural idyll', and to consume it. Their opposition to the economic development of their locality is often premised on the desire to preserve a world that has been lost elsewhere.

Telecommuters

Recent developments and expansion of mass communications (mobile phone, fax, e-mail, electronic file transfer) have made it possible to live on a remote

Scottish island or in an isolated Welsh village and work for a company which is based in London on another metropolitan area. Although there remain problems of network coverage outside the main population concentrations in Britain, increasingly levels of 'working from home' have followed employer promotion of flexible working practices. In the past such work has tended to be of low status and low reward, but it has become increasingly common amongst high-earners in large corporations as well as the more usual freelance media and self-employed workers.

Retired Settlers

Rural areas are proving increasingly popular with retired people. An influx of retired people into Dorset, and Christchurch in particular, between 1971 and 1975 caused the population of these areas to increase by 14 per cent. An important consequence of the influx of retired people is a greater strain on the health services in these areas.

Good-Lifers

The 'Laura Ashley factor' is the reason some people decide to leave the city and move to a rural area (*The Times*, 30 January 1997). Karen MacNee's (1996) research suggests that some migrants who settle on the Island of Skye are 'romantics' who went to Skye for a summer holiday, fell in love with it, and decided to settle there. After spending a winter on Skye a large proportion of these romantics will become disenchanted and leave. Other migrants, MacNee argues, have more realistic expectations of rural life. They are usually middle-class nuclear families who go to Skye with the aim of setting up small, home-based businesses such as guesthouses, craft shops, tea shops, etc.

Study Point
Consider which category you would be likely to fall into if you were to live in the depths of the country: 1 prefer to commute to the nearest big town; 2 telecommute; 3 live in the country only in later retirement; 4 live a simple 'good life'.

SOURCES OF CONFLICT BETWEEN INCOMERS AND LOCALS

Income

The relative affluence of incomers to rural areas is sometimes a source of conflict. In her study of rural Stirling, MacNee (1996) found that 38 per cent of incomers had incomes of over £15,000 per annum, compared with 21 per cent of those who had always lived in the area. It is a level of spending power that cannot be satisfied by local markets, inevitably leading to much consumer activity remaining outside the rural area.

Housing

Housing is an important source of conflict and tension. Commuters and retired people are often attracted to rural areas because they can afford to buy an attractive 'home' (never a house), sometimes with land attached. Local people frequently cannot compete with urban incomers in the housing market because of the generally lower level of rural wages. Incomers to rural areas are more likely to be owner-occupiers than people who have always lived in the area.

Second Homes

The tensions caused by incomers outbidding locals in the housing market are intensified when migrants are buying properties as second homes or holiday homes. These incomers tend to live in town during the working week, only returning to the rural area at weekends or during holidays. This has a distorting effect on the local economy and society. These conflicts are heightened when the urban incomers are of a different nationality to the locals. Organisations in Scotland such as Settler Watch and Scotland Watch and unattached activists in Wales have been accused of intimidation against such migrants, especially second-home owners and other 'outsiders'. The burning of over 100 'English-owned' cottages in Wales since 1979 was satirised by the comedy team of *Not the Nine O'clock News* as 'Come Home to a Real Fire!', parodying an advertisement for coal at the time. To counter this aggression peacefully, but with a similar agenda, Cymdeithas Tai Gwynedd was formed to find homes and work for native Welsh people in rural Wales (Osmond 1988).

Conflicting ideas of rural life

Urban incomers to rural areas often bring with them an idealised vision of rural life. Yet modern farming methods – for example, hedgerow removal, straw burning, crop spraying, to say nothing of farmyard smells, and the noise of agricultural machinery – do not fit easily with their idealised vision of rural life. To quote the English rural sociologist, Howard Newby:

> *The newcomers often possess a set of stereotyped expectations of village life which place a heavy emphasis on the quality of the rural environment ... many newcomers hold strong views on the desired social and aesthetic qualities of the English village. It must conform as closely as possible to the prevailing urban view – picturesque, ancient and unchanging.*

(Newby 1985)

In order to safeguard this idealised image of rural life, middle-class urban incomers become active in heritage bodies such as the National Trust/National Trust for Scotland; English Heritage; Historic Scotland and CADW Wales; in pressure groups such as Common Ground which campaign for local distinctiveness; and in local amenity and preservation groups, many of which were formed between 1955 and 1975 and are dedicated to protecting the character and physical appearance of villages and their surrounding areas (McCrone, Morris, Kiely 1995).

Contrast the demands of modern farm management with the sorts of issues mobilised by environmental pressure groups. Can these people work in harmony? Outline the respective arguments of each group, listing six points for each. Having done that consider, in 50 words, whether tourism and the heritage industry offer the potential for common ground or further conflict.

WHAT IS THE 'LAND'?

Throughout the analysis of changes in land use outlined in this chapter, there lies the notion that the land has primacy. It should be clear that the 'land' is not just a physical category, something to be bought and sold, furrowed and sown. The land has immense ideological power also. In particular the land is important for turning the rural locality into a community, binding its people around the seasons of the agricultural year – the harvest festival, the flower show, the shoot, the hunt, the common ridings, the Young Farmers and Womens' Rural. But the land has also great significance for the nation and for national identity: the cry of motherland and fatherland is the core of the nationalist's rhetoric. The 'land' is therefore as central to creating a sense of community in the rural locality as it is powerful in the imagined community of the nation.

To develop this theme, read the following quote by David McCrone:

> We have grown very used to 'land' being equated with rural affairs, and 'landownership' being a problem of Highland estates well away from where most Scots live. This is not of course to say that most Scots care little about the 'land' question conventionally defined, because there is something fundamental about that question, which connects directly and urgently with political change in our country. Using that word 'country' is part of the clue, for we equate it with 'land' in a very significant way. The Welsh writer, the late Raymond Williams, remarked that 'country' is both a nation and part of a 'land'; the 'country' can be the whole society as well as its rural area. It is 'Country' as well as 'country' (Williams, 1973). Our 'land' is then nicely ambiguous. It refers to the rural parts, but it is also the essence of the 'Country'...
>
> To be sure, this equation of nation with land is not unique to us. The idealisation of most countries is with the land: think of England's green and pleasant land, of 'greenwood freedom', of 'Welsh Wales', the Gaeltachd of both Ireland and Scotland – seen in both cases as the heartland of the culture...

(McCrone 1997)

SUMMARY

The idealised images of rural life painted by Myles Birket Foster and Helen Allingham do not prove an accurate reflection of the countryside today. The British countryside is a changing countryside. The historic clearances of the native woodlands, through the parliamentary enclosures of 1750–1830, to the mechanisation of agriculture and the introduction of set-aside in the twentieth century are all examples of countryside change.

As we approach the end of the twentieth century, the British countryside continues to undergo much development. There are two questions which have to be asked. What kind of countryside do we want to see in the twenty-first century? How can we develop the right kind of policies to ensure that the countryside we get is the countryside that we want?

Rural policies are a product of their time. The vision of rural policy contained in the Scott Report of 1941 is not appropriate for the twenty-first century. Successive governments have been forced to reconsider the future development of rural areas in order to strike a balance between the sometimes competing interests of agriculture, forestry, conservation, recreation, tourism, and rural economic development. The White Papers on Rural England (DoE/MAFF 1955); Rural Scotland (SO 1995); and Rural Wales (Welsh Office 1996) represent an attempt to achieve this aim.

Group work

Divide the class into two separate groups, and consider the following question:

What do we mean by rural life and urban life?

1 Ask members of each group to list the main features of 'rural life' and 'urban life'.

2 The groups should then discuss the similarities and the differences in their lists with the class as a whole, concentrating on the problems and opportunities people in each environment face.

Before constructing your lists, re-read the section in Chapter 2 which presented Tönnies' conceptualisation of two contrasting ways of living: *Gemeinschaft* and *Gesellschaft*. Look at Table 3 on p 13 which explains the terms. Use this model to help identify the dominant features of rural and urban life and, in particular, look for instances when the demands of modern life appear to be clashing with notions of the 'rural idyll'. You could get hold of a property guide for your region, or look at the 'housing for sale' section in any quality national Sunday newspaper. Compare how the estate agents present and offer housing in the country with those in the town.

Coursework

1 'An examination of the action and motives of an environmental pressure group in your area'
Information for this topic will come from your local press and from the literature of local environmental groups. Try to go along to their meetings or interview one of their organisers.

2 'The changing use of the countryside in your region'
Again the local press and the local council may have information for you on this topic. But also get in touch with local farmers and their associations. Perhaps you could visit your local agricultural museum or agricultural college if you have one, or visit a nearby farmer that you have contacted previously.

Exam Hints

Think about what you have learned and understood from this chapter and add it to the knowledge you have gained from Chapter 2. A specimen examination question is given below which links the work of Chapters 2 and 3:

Assess the evidence and arguments which suggest that the traditional distinction between urban and rural communities no longer adequately explains social change in modern societies.

A possible answer to this question would explore the traditional distinction between the urban and the rural community (the rural–urban community, *Gemeinschaft* and *Gesellschaft*, the community study of the village and the town); you might then analyse the conflicting ideals regarding land use in the countryside (the rural idyll in the countryside today, the physical changes in the land use of the British countryside, sources of conflict between incomers and locals in the rural community).

Revision Hints

From this chapter, you should now understand the following themes. Take time to make a key concept card on each:

- The rural idyll.
- The changing physical appearance of the countryside.
- The changing land use structure of the countryside.
- Tourism and the environment.
- The changing social composition of the countryside.
- Sources of conflict between incomers and locals in rural areas.
- The ideological importance of the 'land' to national identity.

Practice Questions

1 To what extent has research by sociologists confirmed or undermined the image of the rural idyll?
2 Outline the major changes in the social composition of the British countryside since 1945. What light has sociological research thrown on the causes and consequences of the changes?

4

CHANGE IN THE CITY

Introduction

THIS CHAPTER EXPLORES what lies behind the notion of the rural–urban continuum, two very distant poles, one urban and one rural. We have seen in Chapter 3 how idealised notions of the country and the rural idyll have been maintained historically and in the present day. Desirable images of what we want or believe the countryside to be in our mind's eye have been divorced from the reality of farming and land management in the late twentieth century. Now our focus turns to the city, and how social and other identities (class, religious and ethnic, for example) have been altered and how new identities have been created. Living in the town and city has been the norm for British society, and for many other societies around the world, since the nineteenth century. From the cathedral city of the shires of England to the shanty towns of Delhi or Mexico City, the urban experience has often been said to have formed and forged a new sense of locality, community and national identity – one quite different from life in the countryside.

Table 5: *Theorists, Concepts and Issues in this chapter*		
KEY THEORISTS	KEY CONCEPTS	KEY ISSUES
Saunders	Theories of urbanisation	What are the classical theories of the city?
Marx	Proletariat	Urban life intensifies class conflict
Durkheim	Functional differentiation	Can urbanisation increase solidarity?
Weber	The city	What are the pre-conditions for any city?
Davis	Urbanisation Measuring the city	The 'proportion' urban and rural When is a village a town, a town a city?

Wirth	Size, density, complexity	Is there a unique urban 'way of life'?
Braudel	'A town is a town'	Is the city a 'generator' of experiences?
Abrams	Reification	Does the city behave like a real person?
The Chicago School	Urban ecology	How is urban land/housing distributed?
Hoyt, Alonso	Sectors and wedges	Refining the concentric ring model
Smith	Housing segregation	How has 'race' affected housing choice?
Gilroy	Ethnic identity	How do ethnic minorities retain cultural values?
Kettle & Hodges	Urban race riots	How do we explain the urban riot?
	Homelessness, slums	Is the urban world collapsing?
Ross	Survival networks	How are urban communities maintained? Are urban communities now undermined? Are the people or the residential area to blame?

CLASSICAL THEORIES

Chapter 2 showed that the town and the city have been central to the theories produced by the founding fathers of sociology. In *Social Theory and the Urban Question* (1986, Hutchinson), Peter Saunders summarises the classical sociological views as follows:

Marx and Engels:

Although the city does not itself create the modern proletariat, it is an important condition for the self-realisation of that group. Its importance is to concentrate the working class to an extent that exacerbates 'their condition' and highlights and enhances the potential of this group for collective self-action.

Durkheim:

He takes urbanisation as an important precondition of the development of functional differentiation in society. Urbanisation creates a new level of more varied and often more autonomous relationships, expressing what is 'abnormal'. Durkheim's concern is to show that, while the development of the division of labour contains within it the stronger basis of social solidarity, it nevertheless comes to be expressed through 'abnormal behaviour'.

Weber:

The medieval city in Europe was the place where the crucial political as well as economic break from feudalism was accomplished. He argues that by analysing the economic and political organisation of the city we are better able to understand it than by thinking in terms of size (i.e. the number of people who live there).

(Saunders, 1986)

These are three different approaches, with implications which go beyond the scope of this study, but they direct us towards the fundamental characteristics of the urban experience – the city is a place where there are many autonomous relationships which can lead either to group solidarity on a mass scale or to personal isolation; in each case the city is the place where modern society was born and sustained.

Study Point
Consider which of the three classical views appeals most strongly to you: 1   City life politicises people, uniting them as a force for change. 2   City life usually highlights the wide variation in social groups, especially the deviant. 3   The city is the source of economic and political power and drives progress forward.

DEFINING URBANISATION

So far we have stressed the importance of the transition from a world that was mainly rural to one where most people live in towns and cities. In spite of all this intense sociological effort to distinguish between rural and urban, it is still not easy to say when the countryside and the village end and, by implication, where towns and cities begin. How do you know when you are in a town or a city?

In reality there is no neat and tidy cut-off point between rural and urban. This is because the transition from a rural to a predominantly urban world, what sociologists call 'urbanisation', is a social and historical process.

Kingsley Davis (1974) has provided a key definition: 'Urbanisation is a proportion of the total population concentrated in an urban settlement, or else a rise in this proportion.'

Urbanisation does not measure the actual growth of cities; it is not about the size of cities. Accordingly, Davis adds, cities can grow without any urbanisation provided that the rural population grows at an equal or a greater rate. Urbanisation is the relative proportion of those in towns. But this still begs the questions, what is a town? and how can we measure it?

Most straightforwardly, size is an important determinant. More people and more families live in a town or city than in a country village – there are more houses and more streets. But how many people do you need? What is the cut-off point between a village and a small town, between a cathedral city and a capital city? When we said that over half the British population were counted as living in urban areas in the census of 1851, that was a measurement of urban areas of 2,000 or more people. Today this figure seems very low, so many towns that we regard as small have 5,000 or 10,000 residents. A higher cut-off point would perhaps gather a more accurate catch, excluding many of the minnows. The United Nations takes 20,000 as a figure, Britain's Census Bureau works with a notion of 'urban area' – a bricks and mortar definition which tries to avoid an exact figure. (For more information, see the census returns for your area in your local library; for national information, contact the Bureau directly, or see: http://census.ac.uk/).

POINTS OF EVALUATION

1 Whatever defining size we choose it can be no more than an arbitrary decision. There can never be a right answer.
2 A figure of 20,000 might be more meaningful for defining the urban experience in England, but be too large for Wales or for northern Scotland, yet far too small for the United States of America.
3 Taking size as an indicator of urbanisation can never provide more than a partial understanding, and this has been recognised by social scientists.

THE BEGINNINGS OF THE CITY

Perhaps the most influential sociological definition of urbanisation has come from Max Weber. In *The City* (1958), Weber identified the features which he then used to define and classify the very beginnings of the city:

- **Fort**: in the medieval sense this means some form of garrison, but for the modern city it translates into control of 'internal violence', ie the police force (or the army in extreme circumstances), or other moral or community control.
- **Market**: generally meaning specialisation in trade products and a regular, not an occasional, exchange of goods. In this sense the whole 'city' is the market because of the constant exchange of goods and services.
- **Court of its own**: Weber states that 'A locale can be held to be a city in a political–administrative sense though it would not qualify as a city economically'. Taken together with 'fort', this enhances self-administration of the urban area.
- **Related form of association**: the appearance of an association of urbanities in contradiction to countrymen; members of local professional associations such as guilds or crafts.
- **Potential autonomy and self-autonomy**: their own administrative districts where those franchised voted for their own form of local government and were policed by those whom they legitimated.

The city, then, is a place of regular and formal economic exchange, of self-administration, and of association.

Examine some university brochures to see how many have the four characteristics of a city:

1   a business involvement;
2   an administrative centre (even a court to deal with students who misbehave);
3   members of professions who operate within it;
4   high levels of autonomy. What conclusions do you draw?

THE CITY AND SOCIETY: SIZE, DENSITY AND HETEROGENEITY

The ideas of Weber are important for helping us understand how cities first grow and how they are maintained throughout history, but our primary interest here is in how the town and city has shaped us as social beings. An important question that theorists have debated is, does living in the town and city change the way we think, or believe, or the way we interact with friends, family and community? These were the concerns of Louis Wirth who expressed his thoughts in an article 'Urbanisation as a way of life' in 1938. His aim was to get to the heart of urban living and in doing so he proposed one of the most influential definitions of urbanisation. He introduced three measurements which, when taken together, explain how living in the town and city shapes us as social actors:

- Size
- Density
- Heterogeneity (or complexity)

The question of size has already been considered, an urban place contains many thousands of people. But do they live very close to each other, or are they spread over many acres? Density is an important measure of urbanity – the depth of urbanisation. In the 1890s there were on average 4,068 people per square mile in the towns compared with 154 in the rural districts (Waller 1983). The Ordnance Survey's *Statistical Atlas of the UK* (1995) defines a metropolitan area as being of 200,00 or more inhabitants and with a population density of 1,000 persons or more per square kilometre. Because of size and because of density, many believe there is a significant difference in experiencing urbanism as a 'way of life'. The difference is linked to the third concept proposed by Wirth – heterogeneity. Otherwise known as complexity, the idea here is that the depth of urbanisation is a reflection of the *number* of social and economic interactions with others that are experienced as well as the logistical and *impersonal* nature of these interactions and the *range* of opportunities for interaction and social activity. We meet more people when going to school or work in the town, although we do not know their names. It takes a long time to drive through the city centre, even though we may be travelling only a few miles. In the city we can buy many kinds of bread, five varieties of tomato and the head-line bands play their concerts. In the village there may be one shop, possibly a part-time post office, and a shared village hall for parish council meetings and for singing carols at Christmas. Life may be complex in the country, and isolating too, especially without private transport, but not of the form and in the number of anonymous interactions which characterise a large and densely packed city centre. Wirth defines a city as 'a relatively large, dense and permanent settlement of socially heterogeneous individuals'.

THE CITY AS A WAY OF LIFE

All the time Wirth is asking the question, what is different about urban living? Does it change who we are? 'Because the city is a product of growth rather than instantaneous creation ... our social life bares the imprint of an earlier folk society. ... Hence we should not expect to find abrupt and discontinuous variation between urban and rural types of personality' (1938).

But still he regards them as two ends of a continuum of ideal types.

Urbanisation no longer denotes merely the process by which persons are attracted to a place called the city. It refers to that cumulative accentuation of the characteristic distinctive of the mode of life which is associated with the growth of cities. ... The question is not whether cities in our civilisation or in others' do exhibit these distinctive traits, but how potent they are in moulding the character of social life into its specific urban form.

(Wirth 1938)

Wirth argues that a characteristic of urban living is the onset of anomie, or absence of norms. This concept, made famous by Durkheim in his work on suicide, tells us about the psychological damage of urban living. It becomes isolating because of the tendency to be physically separated from family and friends. In an example, Wirth asks of the woman who was raped on her way home from a night out in the city, 'where were all her friends?'. They lived a few streets or blocks away, a tube or bus ride away, but they were not physically nearby to help when she called out. Urban life, as Wirth defines it, is an isolating experience. To compensate, we join clubs and societies, neighbourhood watch schemes, playgroups, or go to the leisure centre. The territorial confines of the rural community are replaced by community through 'interest groups'. Urbanism as a way of life means leaving the extended family and the community, and recreating a substitute network throughout the city. This may compensate, and defer anomie, but it suggests that the idea of the community has been lost – a theme we shall return to.

Study Point
List eight ways in which people who live in cities endeavour to create support networks which may previously have been provided by family and kin.

THE CITY AS 'GENERATOR'

The idea that city life makes us act and interact differently must also be emphasised. The image of the city as a generator, speeding up all our interactions, is the powerful metaphor employed by Braudel to explain this phenomenon: 'Towns generate expansion and are themselves generated by it. But even when towns do not create growth from scratch, they undoubtedly channel its course to their own advantage. And growth can be perceived in the towns and cities more clearly than anywhere else' (1985).

Braudel claimed that 'a city is a city wherever it is', because it would display the same characteristics of social life powered by the never-ending generator, and because it exists in a symbiotic or mutually advantageous relationship with the countryside – the town cannot exist on its own without its villages and its rural hinterland. 'Wherever it may be, a town is inseparable from certain realities and processes, certain regular and recurring features'. In particular, he goes on to argue, its highly complex division of labour creates a wide range of specialised occupations, and food is obtained from the market – it is bought – not grown to sustain oneself (Braudel 1985). This is what he means by the fundamental contrast between a town and a village.

Points of Evaluation

1   The historical sociologist Philip Abrams (1978) has criticised Braudel. He accuses him of 'reifying' the city. By this, Abrams means Braudel is treating the city as if it were a living person able to make and impose its own will on others.
2   This is misleading because, as Abrams says, all social changes will then be ascribed *to the city*, and what he regards as more fundamental concepts such as class, gender and race will be ignored.
3   These latter concepts would be important irrespective of the village, the town or the city. It is argued that they are not unique to the city, and so cannot define it.

Activity
Chapter 2 outlined the criticisms of the 'community study' by the sociologists Bell and Newby, who called for the application in a systematic fashion of the fundamental sociological concepts such as class, status and power to the study of social life in rural areas. The community study was non-quantitative and too reliant upon subjective and impressionistic data. They, too, make the point that the community study is reifying parts of the city, just as Abrams has criticised Braudel's approach. To understand this point more fully, and to bring in the argument of Wirth also, write 100 words on whether the city makes us do things that are unique to the urban experience. Take 'joy-riding' as your example (the taking of cars by children and youths, who then race them at high speed before abandoning them). Is this a crime created by the city, or is it symptomatic of wider sociological factors such as poverty, inequality, lack of education?

CHANGE IN THE CITY: LIVING AND WORKING

Every urban area has many land uses – industrial, recreational, commercial, educational – but housing remains the largest single category and the most general. Very few people have complete freedom to choose where they live. Individual decisions on where to live are not taken in a vacuum. We generally don't build our own houses. The overwhelming majority of us select from the limited range of houses available at the time. For those who are poor, this choice is usually limited in the extreme, especially in recent years as local councils systematically diminish their own housing stocks. Throughout the nineteenth century the vast majority of homes were rented: by 1914 about 75–85 per cent of all houses were let by private landlords; by 1971 this had fallen to about 15 per cent; in the 1990s the figure is about 10 per cent.

The housing market never quite behaves as the economists would like. The problem of external factors is always a real one. Two identical houses the same distance from the centre, but one next to a park and the other next to a chemical plant, experience the positive and the negative effect of such externalities which thus affect the value of each house (Morris 1990). The constraints and imperfections of the urban housing market are obvious. Housing does not necessarily lose value as it ages, although it generally does a little, and the trend can be reversed through 'gentrification' or improvement. But the boom and crash in the housing market in 1980s Britain, particularly in England, is an example of the volatility in housing prices which bears no relation to the materials used in the construction of a house or its state of repair. But how should we understand the spread of different housing and of different residential areas in the industrial and modern city? What models can we use to determine the residential concentrations which lie behind urban communities? Geographers have readily employed the land-use models of the Chicago School in which land particular to retail, commercial and residential uses requires sites at varying distances from the central business district.

CONCENTRIC RINGS: THE CHICAGO SCHOOL

The 'Chicago School' of urban analysis produced what has been called probably the most famous diagram in the social sciences: the concentric rings model of urban development. The diagram was based on Chicago in the early part of the twentieth century. We have adapted it for the British example – see p 46.

Study Point

Consider the area in which you live. Does it have the features suggested by the Chicago School? Are any clearly absent? Why might this be the case?

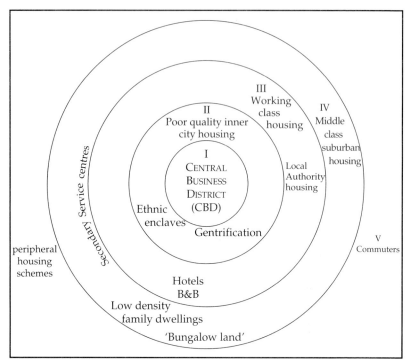

CONCENTRIC RINGS OF THE CHICAGO SCHOOL (DERIVED FROM BURGESS, 1925)

Rather than studying housing types and areas – a morphological approach to urban change – the Chicago School stressed the need to study its society, an approach termed 'human ecology'. This is a study of people in relation to their environment.

Burgess's ideal type of city structure, the concentric rings model shown above, was the logical outcome of this approach. The ecologists claimed that social relations are formed out of spatial relations, such as residential choice. Basically, if a poor family is rehoused in an inner-city area for problem families then they too, in turn, will be tarred with the same brush.

Points of Evaluation

1 The concentric rings model has been refined by Homer Hoyt who introduced 'sectors' and 'wedges' which cut across the concentric rings. Writing in the late 1930s, Hoyt became convinced that residential growth in American cities was more axial than concentric (Badcock 1984).

2 In a similar way, the sociologist William Alonso brought this theory forward by introducing into the equation the user's ability to pay rent (Ley 1983). Both Hoyt and Alonso have based their conceptualisation of the internal geography of the city on a *filtering down* of the housing stock between the classes.

3 This filtering down of the housing stock is seen as the mechanism by which small status and social differences are worked out in the housing market to produce identifiably separate residential areas in the industrial city. These produce, Hoyt and Alonso would claim, a compromise in the concentric rings model: with these rings being cut across by sectors and zones. They suggest as their compromise that social class and the affordability of rent produces 'sectors', and household/family decision based around the life-cycle are 'zonal'.

Activity

How appropriate is this analysis to the British example? From your knowledge of London today, or from another large city, identify the relevance (or not) of the following features:

- concentric rings of housing types around a central business district;
- sectors or wedges of particular housing type based on social class or kinship groups;
- the importance of the 'east end' and the 'west end' to the structure of the British city.

URBANISATION AND RACE

RACE AND HOUSING

The examples considered so far have concentrated on the distribution of housing and urban communities as they have been created by inequalities in income and wealth, or social class. Yet these issues are complicated further when we look at the distribution of housing, and the urban community, according to race. The work of the human geographer Susan J. Smith has shown that 'segregation is not a neutral expression of cultural preference'. Rather, she argues, racial inequality is in the labour market, in access to housing and in many areas of social opportunity.

Only 3 per cent of black people (in contrast to the national average of 24 per cent) live in rural enumeration districts, and three-quarters live in a set of urban enumeration districts containing just 10 per cent of all whites (Brown 1984). This means that about half the white population lives in a neighbourhood containing no black residents …

(Smith, 1989)

Points of Evaluation

1   Much segregation exists *within* immigrant communities, especially Asian and Afro-Caribbean, as well as *between* them (Smith 1989).

2   It is notable that there is little spread, if any, out to white areas. Instead there seems to be a steady increase in density in these black neighbourhoods.

3   In many ways the position of black people is not helped by their over-representation in lower paid jobs and in the statistics of those out of work.

Study Point

Make three tables from the data provided by Brown, above, to show:

1   the percentage of black people living in rural enumeration districts contrasted with the national average;
2   the percentage of black people living in these areas contrasted with white people;
3   the percentage of white people living in neighbourhoods in which there are no black people.

RACE AND COMMUNITY

In addition to housing and employment distribution, race is important when it comes to understanding how cultural and national identities are both forged and maintained. In the words of Paul Gilroy: 'Races are not, then, simple expressions of either biological or cultural sameness. They are imagined – socially and politically constructed – and the contingent processes from which they emerge may be tied to equally uneven patterns of class formation to which they, in turn, contribute' (1996).

Gilroy's work has concentrated on those of West Indian origin and how they create an ethnic community. His particular interest is in how minority ethnic groups maintained or abandoned a distinctive culture in the face of a larger 'official' culture. Important and influential as it is, Gilroy's work has been criticised for ignoring non Afro-Caribbeans who are described, generically, as black. Modood (1994) has argued that there is a danger in using 'colour' as a determinant of terminology: 'many race relations battles turn on issues of culture and minority rights as on colour discrimination and socio-economic deprivation'.

This difference in cultural beliefs between the ethnic groups labelled as 'black' should be borne in mind, as should the differences within each of the groupings themselves, as Table 6 shows.

	ENGLAND AND WALES (%)*				
Table 6: *Participation of young people in selected leisure activities, January 1993*			PAKISTANI/ OTHER ETHNIC		
	BLACK	INDIAN	BANGLADESHI	MINORITIES	WHITE
Party, night-club, disco	49	39	20	43	64
Cinema, theatre, concert	48	46	25	46	48
Used computer for pleasure	36	48	33	47	47
Participated in sports activity	24	36	23	38	39
Attended religious service, etc.	22	36	25	32	12
Meal in restaurant	21	39	18	27	38
Visited a public house	16	26	3	26	66
Hung around near home	15	15	8	19	17
Went to an amusement arcade	14	20	7	9	9
Watched a live sports event	12	24	15	17	21
Played a musical instrument	11	11	6	11	18
Hung around in city centre	10	19	11	16	17
Youth club, etc.	9	9	11	12	13
Did community work	6	8	6	11	7
Attended a political meeting, etc.	4	1	3	2	3

*PERCENTAGE AGED 14–25 WHO HAD PARTICIPATED IN EACH ACTIVITY IN THE MONTH BEFORE INTERVIEW. SOURCE: YOUTH LIFESTYLES SURVEY, HOME OFFICE, *OFFICE OF NATIONAL STATISTICS: SOCIAL FOCUS ON ETHNIC MINORITIES* (1996) LONDON: HMSO

These are important subtleties in our analysis, yet too easily overlooked. That they get ignored in the debate around race, housing, community and society, can be seen from an examination of the most serious urban riots in recent British history.

Activity
Martin Kettle and Lucy Hodges (1982, *Uprising!* Pan Books, London) explain the events of the Brixton riots of April 1981. Your task is to evaluate in 100–200 words the various responses given as explanations of these events: • **A law-and-order issue**: The immediate response was that 'nothing can justify it'; it was caused by a weakening of personal social discipline, especially in the schools.

- **Outsiders, conspirators and copycats**: The common theme was the disbelief that the communities could be capable of such acts as riots against themselves, with a denial of the race issue.
- **The racial dimension**: 'Organised skinheads'; but otherwise a general reluctance to discuss this as an issue.
- **Deprivation and unemployment**: The rioting took place in 'decaying central areas of old cities where there is intolerably high unemployment, unacceptably low levels of social services and abysmally inadequate housing'.

Points of Evaluation

1 The events of 1981 were perhaps the closest the British city has ever come to replicating the inherent problem of the race ghetto which characterises many of the large American cities.
2 They were also a reminder that perhaps the slum of the nineteenth century had not gone away. The housing stock may have improved in terms of its basic amenities, but the inner city was being left to a multiply-disadvantaged underclass, one that was over-represented by Britain's ethnic minorities.
3 The problem had been compounded by an increase in the number of homeless people, in London and all of the larger urban centres.
4 The extent of homelessness (Table 7) in comparison with other nations of Europe has given rise to fears that British cities are becoming either American-style ghettos or resembling the shanty towns of the third word.

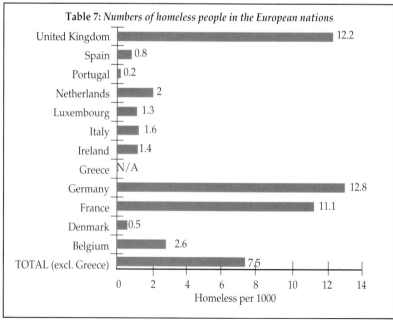

Table 7: *Numbers of homeless people in the European nations*

Nation	Homeless per 1000
United Kingdom	12.2
Spain	0.8
Portugal	0.2
Netherlands	2
Luxembourg	1.3
Italy	1.6
Ireland	1.4
Greece	N/A
Germany	12.8
France	11.1
Denmark	0.5
Belgium	2.6
TOTAL (excl. Greece)	7.5

SOURCE: OECD (1996) TABLE 4.2

5   The low socio-economic status of many inner city areas has led to suggestions by Sudjic (1992) and others that the urban community is no more. Fragmented social relationships, limited economic opportunity and monotonous leisure time have, it is argued, replaced integrated residential areas of extended kin and a social life based around home, church and work.
6   These problems are not confined to the inner cities. In Britain, low quality housing on the edge of cities, especially the high rise flats of the 1960s and 1970s, has come increasingly to the fore as an issue in urban analysis.

THE URBAN COMMUNITY

The examples we have so far shown suggest that the community ideal has been lost forever in the city of today. It would seem that dislocations in society, including homelessness, urban deprivation and racial segregation, point to the end of community. This theme can be considered by comparing two descriptions of the urban community; one in the years following the First World War, the other (on p 52) more recent:

Working class self-help took many forms. Groups of male co-workers often took collections to provide for a man's illness, his funeral, or for his widow and orphans, using such procedures as work-place or pub 'whip-rounds'. 'Slate-clubs', often pub-sponsored, were a slightly more formalised method of raising money for emergencies. Most neighbourhood-based self-help was organised through women, but involved men too, especially shopkeepers and boy children ... Mrs Barnes, whose husband provided her with a very scanty income, sold cooked sheep's heads and pigs' feet from a stall outside the Britannia Theatre in Hoxton, a business in which she had been helped by the local butcher.

'... Everybody knew the children belonged to the Nichol and everybody was kind to the children. There was hardly any traffic – the children could go anywhere and had no fear of anything. The coal carts didn't go fast. The chimney sweeps, they knew everybody. And so the result was a close-knit community and everybody knew everybody.'

(Ross 1983)

Activity
Undertake a short piece of research to discover the different views a sample of people have about the meaning of 'neighbourhood' and 'community'.

HOME OFFICE

Press Release 21/9/97   *9 September 1997*

HOME SECRETARY LAUNCHES PLANS FOR SAFER COMMUNITIES
IN COVENTRY AND NEWARK

Local communities in the Midlands will be safer from anti-social behaviour, Home
Secretary Jack Straw announced today.

Mr Straw visited Coventry and Newark today as part of his 'Tackling Youth Crime
and Disorder' tour this month. He met local residents, police, social services,
probation officers and community representatives to hear about local problems and
new initiatives.

During his visit, the Home Secretary unveiled plans for a new Community Safety
Order, which will give courts powers to impose strict conditions on people whose
anti-social behaviour causes innocent people distress or fear.

Coventry was one of the first authorities in the country to try to take out injunctions
against residents. When their attempts failed for legal reasons, they called for new
powers and Community Safety Orders to be introduced.

He also welcomed plans for a new multi-agency initiative, 'Reclaiming Coventry'
designed to improve the quality of life for residents in targeted areas of the city.

'Reclaiming Coventry' will focus on targeting and tackling community safety issues
and will be backed up by social support and environmental improvement schemes.

The operation will be led principally by the Community Action Against Crime
Team, working with local residents and other agencies including: the police, Victim
Support, Coventry Drugs Team and Coventry and Warwickshire Community
Safety Scheme.

(Central Office of Information at http://www.labour.org.uk/news/index.html.)

Activity
Compare the two extracts from Ross and the Central Office of Information and write 200–300 words which debate whether the urban community has now been lost forever.

SUMMARY

Urbanisation is the most common residential experience today, yet it is not the
easiest to understand. Ensure that you have made a list of the positions
advocated by the main theorists of urbanisation and be sure to place them in the
context of your wider sociological knowledge. Take care not to treat the city as if

it were a human person (to reify it). Contrast the urban community with the rural examples you have discussed already, and see how this fits with the changing use of land discussed in the previous chapter. Take account of the importance of race for cutting across many of the social variables that we use. It is a fundamental influence, too, on national identity.

Group work

In large part the 'end of community' debate is between 'physical locality' and 'society': which is the stronger determinant on our behaviour? Take this theme in greater detail, using the source as an example. Divide the class into two groups. Group A should take the position of a local councillor, Group B should take on the role of resident. How can an area such as the one described ever be 'improved'?

Bulldozers are to be sent in to demolish a Glasgow housing blackspot eight years after £1 million was spent on a refurbishment. Vandals have forced councillors to cut their losses on the South Balornock estate, which won an architectural award as a prime example of Scottish urban regeneration. The vandals have reduced the showcase to a shambles. Where houses had been extensively refurbished and a children's playground formed a colourful centrepiece, all that remains are gutted, roofless shells and a rubble-strewn eye-sore ... A report before yesterday's housing management meeting told of intimidation, drug dealing, burglaries and assaults. ... When potential new tenants viewed the properties, fewer than one in ten accepted the council's offer. The small minority willing to accept soon changed their minds following what the report termed 'abuse and threats from a criminal element present in the area. The area has become virtually impossible to let during the past year as its reputation has worsened.'

(The Scotsman, 16 October, 1997)

Coursework

1 'A comparison of popular images of the rural idyll and the inner city'
  Your starting point should be Raymond Williams's important work *The Country and the City* (1973). Newspapers, magazines, advertisements, tourist

board information and reports commissioned by your local council are all likely to be useful sources of evidence. You could also take some photographs yourself.

2 'An examination of the modern suburb on the outskirts of a small or medium-sized town'

Visit your local town or city archive or planning office to get information on the development of such a suburb. Look also in local newspapers and for the publications of local history groups to examine the development of housing estates in your area. If time and resources allow, devise a questionnaire to gather information on the socio-economic profile of the suburb, concentrating on where the residents locate their employment.

Exam Hints

Assess sociological explanations of social problems and social conflict in cities.

A possible answer to this question would outline social problems and conflicts such as residential patterns segmented by social class, race and housing, alienation and anomie in the city. You could then introduce the following theories: theories of urbanisation (the Chicago School), Paul Gilroy and black culture, the Brixton Riots, Louis Wirth and urbanism as a way of life.

Revision Hints

From this chapter, you should now understand the following themes. Take time to make a key concept card on each:

- The theories of urbanisation and how the main theorists have conceptualised it.
- Wirth's 'urbanism as a way of life'.
- Reification.
- The Chicago School and human ecology.
- Externalities.
- Change in the urban community over time.
- Race and housing; notorious areas.
- Homelessness.

Practice Questions

1 Explain what sociologists mean by the process of urbanisation. Discuss the findings of research studies which have examined the consequences of city life.
2 Critically examine the attempts by sociologists to analyse cities by producing models and theories which define their significant social characteristics.

5

WHEN COUNTRY MEETS CITY

Introduction

CHAPTER 2 SHOWED HOW, for the early sociologists, the idea of the rural-urban continuum was a useful tool for understanding the great changes that had been brought about by the Industrial Revolution and by the French Revolution. We outlined the historical development of the rural–urban continuum and showed how it was thought of as a line running between two poles – the rural at one end, the urban pole at the other.

Since the late nineteenth century there have been a number of attempts by both academics and policy-makers to reconcile the country and the city. The most important of these are:

- suburbanisation;
- 'model' employer housing;
- the garden city movement;
- the small town idyll;
- the urban village;
- 'edge city'.

We will discuss all of these attempts to reconcile the country and the city, and then move to an explanation of why the rural-urban continuum is of increasingly less relevance in the late twentieth century. Instead postmodernity has placed the big historical questions of 'who are we?' and 'where do we come from?' formly on the agenda of everyday life. This has shifted and even merged rural and urban identities. An important by-product of this is that people have been forced to consider and reflect on their national identities too. What, for example, does it mean to be English, Scottish, Welsh and Northern Irish in the late twentieth century? In this way Chapter 5 acts as a bridge between the first and second halves of this book.

Table 8: *Theorists, concepts and issues in this chapter*		
KEY THEORISTS	KEY CONCEPTS	KEY ISSUES
Wiener	Anti-urbanism/ruralism	Why a rejection of modern urbanisation?
Dyos and Reeder	Suburbanisation	When did working class suburbanisation begin? Did it damage the inner city?
Waller/Sutcliffe	Model and garden villages	Why employer paternalism?
Howard	The garden city	Why was 'town-country' seen to be the best?
Geddes	Megalopolis Conurbation	Of what value are these terms coined to describe modern urban growth?
	Small/cathedral towns Ecology and the city	Why did rural preservationists appear and why a concern with historic/ civic roots?
Palen & London	Gentrification	Has the city centre been revitalised?
Coupland	Docklands	Good or bad for the urban community?
Davis	The ecology of fear	New fears and new controls in the city.
Valentine	Dangerous areas	Do men and women have unequal 'spatial opportunities' in the city?
Garreau	Edge city	Is the 'edge city' the future for urban planning?

THE BEGINNING OF THE END FOR THE CITY?

'By the gains of industry we promote art' was the banner at the entrance of Birmingham's Art Gallery, funded by profits from the municipal gas supply (A. Briggs (1968) *Victorian Cities*, Penguin). In mid- to late-nineteenth century Britain there was a counter-reaction to urban growth. Deviance and decay had given rise to strong feelings of 'anti-urbanism'. The thatched cottage with roses growing around the door was held as an ideal, in stark contrast to the horror and disease of shock cities such as Manchester and Middlesborough in the early phases of their growth. This ideal was, quite clearly, the extreme opposite from all that industrialisation and urbanisation stood for.

THE DECLINE OF INDUSTRIAL CAPITALISM

Doubts were beginning to be raised over the moral value of rapid industrialisation and its consequence of rapid urbanisation. John Stuart Mill, the philosophical radical, had difficulty reconciling the demand of being a gentleman with the concerns of material life in mid-Victorian society:

> *I confess I am not charmed with the ideal of life held out by those who think that the normal state of human beings is that of struggling to get on; that the trampling, crushing, elbowing, and treading on each other's heels which forms the existing type of social life, are the most desirable lot of human kind, or anything but the disagreeable symptoms of one of the phases of industrial progress.*
>
> *(Quoted in Wiener 1981)*

Charles Dickens started off as the great supporter of all that was modern – all that was associated with the progress of industrialisation. But this changed as he reflected on the money-making capitalists and the misery and ill-health their methods caused the urban dwellers. In *Hard Times* he associated all that was bad with industrialisation.

There developed, as we saw in Chapter 3, a harking back to the country life and to the days before industrialisation and before modernisation. Whereas the initial urban explosion had drawn attention to the present and the future, by the close of the nineteenth century the old world had been called upon to redress the balance of the new – to legitimate and to provide relief from the stresses of the present.

> *Forget the counties overhung with smoke,*
> *Forget the snorting steam and piston smoke,*
> *Forget the spreading of the hideous town,*
> *Think rather of the pack-horse on the down,*
> *And dream of London, small, and white, and clean.*
> *The clear Thames bordered by its garden green…*
>
> *(William Morris 1870, quoted in Waller 1985))*

Out of the midst of the new urban society 'ruralism' rose up reborn. Anti-urbanism exists just as strongly in the late twentieth century. It takes a variety of forms, for example:

- Prettiest Village competitions
- Village in Bloom competitions
- People owning cottages in rural areas as second/holiday homes
- People choosing to live in the country and either work from home or commute to work in the city on a daily/weekly basis
- Pubs and hotels in towns given names like the Plough, the Wheatsheaf, the Drover.

Activity
Visit your library to see if there are any local histories of villages and towns in your area which show them as they were in the Victorian or Edwardian period. Consider the major changes revealed in photographs and postcards. Sample a local urban area and establish the number of pubs, homes, hotels which have a rural name attached to them.

RECONCILING THE COUNTRY AND THE CITY

SUBURBS: MODIFYING THE URBAN EXPERIENCE

Probably the most significant response to the negative externalities of urban growth, as outlined in Chapter 4, was suburbanisation. The suburb is by its very definition away from the city, that it is on the periphery. Its earliest phase in Britain was to be socially exclusive, followed by the attraction of the wider middle class, the petite bourgeoisie and then the creation of peripheral estates for the working class as well as other commuter nodes. Suburban estates such as Edgbaston or Bloomsbury created exclusivity through their leasehold restrictions, where certain trading and other 'dirty' activities were banished. Planners and residents also constructed fences, planted trees, and promoted their gardens as 'defences' against the outside world. This complemented larger-scale boundaries such as gatehouses on the estate entrance, elite resistance to the siting nearby of tram stations (fearing the lowering of the social status of the area), and the building of parks and botanic gardens, forming a green and pleasant version of barbed wire.

Yet this process works in two ways. Dyos and Reeder (1973) have argued that middle-class economic power itself contributed to the adverse inner-city conditions from which the middle class fled, by deriving an income from renting out the slums, and by redirecting business profits away from environmental improvements in the centre into housing investments in the suburbs. This in turn encouraged working-class suburbanisation. This migration of the working class to the suburbs had always been resisted because of the cost of transport in relation to a working-class wage, and the need to be in the central business district or the docks to pick up casual employment at a time in the morning not served by public transport. Yet with the extension of cheap travel in the 1880s, a ring of working-class suburbs began to circle London and the other metropolitan centres. For example, the population of Leyton increased from 9,000 in 1850 to 98,000 in 1891. West Ham increased from 19,000 to 276,000 in the same period. This trend was common to most large towns, although at a slower pace and generally not so far out from the centre (2–3 miles maximum) as middle-class suburbanisation.

MODEL VILLAGES AND THE GARDEN VILLAGE

Suburbanisation was an attempt to obtain lower urban densities by a conscious escape from the central areas. The aspiring ruralism of its residents was, in the main, led by the middle class. Yet there was also a move to bring the best of the country to the city, in this case it was for the working classes and white collar workers. Edward Arkroyd, a successful Halifax worsted manufacturer, built two model villages at Copely (1849–53) and, more notably, at Arkroydon (1859). They were deemed 'model' because they represented an attempt to engineer, socially as much as architecturally, better social behaviour and a more environmentally uplifting lifestyle. Arkroyd argued that, 'A clean, fresh, well-ordered house exercises on its inmates a moral no less than a physical influence, and has the direct tendency to make the members of the family sober, peaceable, and considerate of the feelings and happiness of each other …'.

These were built as villages for the working class of the factories. The best-known of this mid-century phase of employer housing was Saltaire, the creation of the Bradford manufacturer Tutus Salt. His mill was opened in 1853 and over the next ten years he built 805 cottages in long parallel terraces. Salt had, in fact, carried out a survey of his employees' needs, and built a variety of different sized cottages to meet the requirements of families with different numbers of children and with different income levels.

The next phase of employer house building came in the 1880s and 1890s: the garden village. This model of cheap, lightly constructed housing with an open layout seemed to offer a healthy and uplifting environment, even to working men (Sutcliffe 1981). This was manifest in the 'factory village'. At Port Sunlight, near Birkenhead, the Congregationalist soap manufacturer, William Hesketh Lever, began in 1888 to build a community close to his factory. Lever's Port Sunlight tried to get away from the montomy of box housing and grid-iron settlements – with curved streets and spacious ground. Another example is Bournville, the workers' village for the Cadbury factories. Yet it it worth noting in passing that the vast majority of Bournville residents did not work at the factory (there were over 1000 houses by 1914).

All these examples were approaches to solving the persistent problems of industrial life by trying to build ideal housing in country settings. The very rationale of New Earswick, the village of the rival confectioners and social investigators, Rowntree, was to forge the belief of country life, in an urban location, from a free, organic plan. It grew out of the needs of the users and the nature of the site and, especially, the conviction that living rooms should face the sun. This was a philosophy which was to reach its peak in the garden city movement at the turn of the century.

To understand the ideology behind the factory village, try to view the 1931 film of Port Sunlight. A video cassette has been made from this film and can be borrowed from the North West Film Archive at Manchester Metropolitan University (full details at the end of this book).

WHEN COUNTRY MEETS CITY: THE GARDEN CITY MOVEMENT

The ideals of the garden-city pioneers, architects Raymond Unwin (1863–1940) and Barry Parker (1867–1947), included a renewed attention to the importance of tradition, nostalgia for the Middle Ages, and a devotion to the village as the symbol of the 'natural' way of life they sought to restore. They designed Rowntree's model dwelling at New Earswick in York.

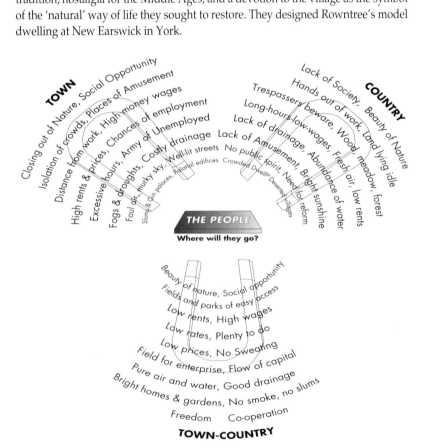

THE THREE MAGNETS (FROM HOWARD, 1902)

Unwin and Parker followed the ideals of of Ebenezer Howard, author of *Tomorrow: A Peaceful Path to Real Reform* (1889), re-issued as *Garden Cities of Tomorrow* in 1902, Howard's theme was a simple one: that town and country must be brought together so that the benefits of both could be enjoyed. This could be achieved by the creation of garden cities, low density housing with green belts and separate industrial and agricultural areas. The ultimate ideal was to recreate the pre-modern community through the correct mix of social classes in a grouping of medium-sized and balanced townships. Howard believed that the evils of overpopulated cities and depopulated countryside were linked, and as a linked problem should be tackled together. His proposal was to create ready-made towns.

Points of Evaluation

1   Howard's ideal town size was 32,000. Welwyn Garden City and Letchworth were attempts to foster a mixture of classes. The intention was to confine city-space into small plots of one-third of an acre and to divide the rest into small farms and allotments, supplying fruit, vegetable and dairy products. There was also a site for industry and a railway link (Waller 1983).

2   Perhaps inevitably the social classes did not mix, and the outcome was the quite typical pattern of class segregation seen in Chapter 4. Some of the residents put up walls, similar occupations gathered together. Status and snobbery overcame utopian harmony – one area in the south-west of Letchworth was called Snob's Hill – and the working class congregated around the factory just as they had done in the large industrial cities.

3   Yet, as Waller makes clear, there was never a representative social mix in the first place. It was the lower middle class and the middle class in general who tended to move to the garden cities rather than the working class (and this should be no surprise from the ideology we have so far presented). Moreover, the garden cities tended to lack the necessary investment in the heterogeneity of their town centres. The utopian intermixing of different classes and the intermixing of urban/industrial and rural/agricultural pursuits was never fully realised. It can be argued that both Welwyn and Letchworth would have failed completely but for their rescue by the government post-1945 when granted the special status of 'New Towns', so enabling much needed infrastructural finance to complete their physical and social development.

Study Point

Consider the way in which the area in which you live or study is socially divided. Are there clearly divided areas in which different classes are likely to be found? Account for this pattern.

THE SMALL TOWN AND THE CATHEDRAL TOWN

The ideology behind these examples is clear and it continues to inform many sections of society: the small town is the ideal urban environment. New life has in recent years been breathed into the old market and cathedral towns. In part this was done by attempts to reconcile the existence of the town with tradition – placing it in a long historical frame with a 'historical pedigree'. The country site has to be repopulated and reinvigorated financially and infrastructurally if, it was argued, a balance between town and country, now lost, was to be re-established. The country town (and the cathedral town) were upheld not only as places of ideal environment, but of importance because they had managed to hang on to their local government and were at the beck and call of no-one. They were in charge of their own affairs and the county town was believed to be the essential English urban type: the basic building block of English/British society (Waller 1983). The love affair with the country in late nineteenth-century Britain was reflected in the formation of a wide range of societies dedicated to protecting the countryside, such as the National Trust for Places of Historic Interest and Natural Beauty (1894), British Empire Naturalists' Association (1905) and the Society for the Promotion of Nature Reserves (1912).

This preservationist concern was an integral part of the late Victorian and Edwardian intellectual reaction to many of the central ideas of economic liberalism. It is no coincidence, for example, that some of the social philosophers and writers in the vanguard of this reaction, such as John Stuart Mill, John Ruskin, William Morris and Thomas Huxley were founder-members of preservationist groups. This profound shift in opinion, with its rejection of the need to constantly improve and become more efficient, arose from a reassessment of the social and economic changes of the nineteenth century – all fuelled by the moral and aesthetic reaction to the urban condition. As we saw in Chapter 3, 'new lifers' have embraced heritage bodies such as the National Trust and Historic Scotland as their means of preserving this past. The optimism and belief in the boundless prosperity that characterised the early growth has been displaced by pessimism about the prospects for social and economic advance.

Study Point
What are some of the pros and cons of preserving areas and special buildings in a town or city? Is it justifiable to protect old telephone boxes or architecture of the recent past?

COUNTRY IN THE CITY, CITY IN THE COUNTRY

The fear of the sort of urban growth just examined produced many responses: some fled the city, some offered new plans to reinvigorate the centre (primarily through relocating the community ideal). We have argued here that suburbanisation was a rural-urban compromise: the distaste for city life – trying to recreate a rural idyll within commuting distance of the city core. Yet some of its former advocates were beginning to see the suburb as an artificial creation – a mere apology for nature in which urban attitudes and values were still dominant. We need to be aware of the extent to which urbanism became a way of life, and of the extent to which it was tempered by this rejection of the economic principles upon which urbanism was based. Since the very beginning, industrialisation has produced popular reaction which have been partly *nostalgic* for the disappearing, pre-industrial world; partly *apocalyptic*, fearing social collapse; and partly *utopian* in seeking to recreate community and social solidarity out of the dislocation and fragmentation brought by industrialisation.

Point of Evaluation

1   As cities in Britain have grown, and as conurbations have been created, many have chosen to commute to work and many more live in 'bungalow land' or peripheral schemes of high-rise developments.
2   These are attempts to combine cheap land and housing costs with a rejection of the density and heterogeneity of urban life.
3   Either way, urbanism as a way of life has forced many to flee to the countryside in search of *Gemeinschaft*. The countryside and the rural idyll still exert a powerful influence in planning the modern town and city today.

ECOLOGY AND THE CITY

The 'ecological balance' of the town and city is a concern which is growing amongst urban planners. In part this means the provision of recycling skips, council amenity sites, and a thorough system of street cleaning and waste removal with 'environmentally friendly' waste storage or recycling. But there is also concern to avoid the 'concrete brutalism' of the 1960s and 1970s and which characterises many New Towns and High Street refurbishments of that time. Rather, there is an impetus to emphasise the historical past of the village, town or city, and do so in a way that complements its rural hinterland. For example, the Local Plan in Cheltenham in the 1980s stressed a concern with conservation:

[The] character of the town is recognised as having national as well as local significance. The Plan seeks to maintain this character in a number of ways: by restricting the future growth of the town, by protecting and enhancing important open spaces and historical buildings, by improving areas or sites which are run down or unattractive, and by endeavouring to ensure that any new development is of a high standard of design and harmonises with existing buildings.

(Quoted in Cowan 1990)

It is argued that this concern has reached its extreme in attempts to regenerate old and decayed parts of city centres and turn them into desirable residential areas. This process is called 'gentrification'.

Study Point
Consider the arguments for and against trying to revitalise poor areas, in which there was a strong working class community, by redeveloping property so that it becomes more expensive and more desirable.

GENTRIFICATION

Turning history into 'heritage' is an important imperative behind the political will to re-develop the city centre. Another important approach is gentrification, and it was one promoted much more by the property developer than by civic or amenity groups, and not necessarily spurred on by local government planners although they are often beneficiaries.

It is argued by Palen and London (1984) that:

• We cannot take gentrifications just to mean neighbourhood revitalisation.
• This process of jostling for urban space is not just upper-status groups replacing lower-status groups in areas of decline in the centre. This 'reinvasion', they suggest, is often accompanied by conflict.
• The effect of gentrification is to 'overheat' the house prices of inner-city areas, stopping the perpetuation of local communities. It can even lead to displacement of lower-income residents as property is condemned, razed to the ground, and office developments and expensive chic housing put in its place. This is a particular feature of the waterside development of former dock sites such as in London, Liverpool and Leith.

LEITH DOCKS DEVELOPMENT

- In many ways the whole process is analogous to the problem of local affordable houses in many villages within commuting distance of large urban centres, or where second homes are bought by 'outsiders' (Chapter 3). The regeneration of the city is the major claim of proponents of this type of development. Yet in each case, it is argued, older communities are displaced and followed by a fragmentation of social class cohesion of the city in the long run.

- Gentrification is not really the revitalisation of the city centre, since some of the working-class communities may already have been 'vital' in any case. On the other hand, many were not 'vital' and gentrification on a small scale has had a successful impact on previously derelict warehouses and mills.

The largest example of this process of gentrification is the Docklands scheme in London. It combines office and residential development in the East End. In many ways its controversial status is a product of its sheer scale, and the need for the British government to bail out the private developers after a crash in property prices in the late 1980s. Yet we should examine it here as a planned response to the decay of the city centre. The question to be asked is, 'has Docklands revitalised London's East End?'.

Activity

What has been the lasting effect of the Docklands development on the East End of London? Its foundations were laid in 1988, and there was much pride in producing the tallest building in Britain. Yet Docklands, according to Coupland (1992), is a controversial development because:

- it was not targeting local unemployment – office jobs were created, but they were not suitable for the low qualifications held by most people in the area;
- it needed increasing amounts of public money to keep it financially viable;
- the housing developed has been too expensive for the local community.

Your task is to evaluate the pros and cons of this development or of a similar waterside programme of regeneration near you.

WHEN CITY MEETS COUNTRY: URBAN FEAR

Dockland development, and the process of gentrification, have been promoted as an answer to the population decline of city centres, and similar proposals can be seen throughout the developed world. Yet it is also part of a wider agenda for dealing with social dislocation in the city. Urban fear has been manifested in many different ways. The overrepresentation of poverty-stricken ethnic minorities in poor quality housing in the centre, the classic American ghetto, are sources of tension witnessed in Chapter 4. Yet they are part of a wide fear of urban apocalypse – social collapse – in the most extreme scenarios, particularly in the largest cities in the world.

Take, for example, the ideas of Mike Davis (1994), who weaves a tale of everyday urban protection, with which we are all familiar, with predictions for a complete urban melt-down. The cult film *Blade Runner*, directed by Ridley Scott, is his starting point: 'Enormous neon images float like clouds above fetid, hyper-violent street, while a voice intones advertisements for extra-terrestrial suburban living in "Off world". Deckard, post apocalypse Philip Marlowe, struggles to save his conscience, and his women, in an urban labyrinth ruled by evil bio-tech corporations …'.

Davis redraws the Chicago School's concentric rings model (Chapter 4, page 46). That model, as we argued, is founded on notions of human ecology which echo social Darwinism, where urban distribution was forged on the lines of the survival of the fittest. We have adapted Davis's stylisation of the American post-industrial city for a British case-study:

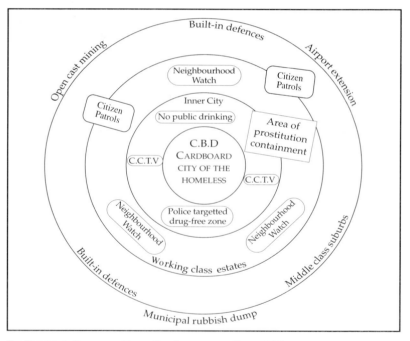

THE ECOLOGY OF FEAR IN THE BRITISH CITY (DERIVED FROM DAVIS, 1995)

Davis uses the term 'scanscape' to describe an obsession with personal safety, especially over inner-city riots. This is a general development where designing safety in the construction of housing is more important than, say, an ecologically efficient heating and insulation system. The provision of Closed Circuit TV (CCTV) has come to be the norm in town and city centres throughout this country and elsewhere.

Beyond the scanscape of Los Angeles and the 'fortified core' are the surrounding ghettoes. Here the fear is of teenage street gangs and, in that city, the sign 'protected by Smith & Wesson' is displayed on many a residence. In Britain handguns are banned but, as in America, the use of private security firms guarding cooperative or sheltered housing, and groups of citizens patrolling their own neighbourhoods are not unusual.

As Davis points out, the ethnic enclaves in the Burgess model have now become 'social control districts'. The most common in Britain's cities are against prostitution or drinking in public. But this is also accompanied by high profile police and media campaigns against drugs and the rave scene. Drug-free zones, particularly in certain night-clubs and other venues, are often a community's immediate response to drug-related deaths amongst youths.

One of the most popular developments in personal security in recent years has been the neighbourhood watch scheme. Organised by a community police officer, the scheme offers meetings to discuss community security, signposting of a 'neighbourhood watch area', stickers and posters, free marking of valuable goods, and a general commitment to look after the property and well-being of your neighbour. These schemes tend to generate a strong sense of community spirit when first established. Yet Davis, amongst others, has doubted the worth of protection through 'circling the wagon train'. It often works as a busybody's charter, or just the opposite in that after a few months the ringing alarms of houses and cars are just ignored or castigated as noise pollution.

Study Point
List the major differences which emerge from a comparison of the concentric ring model with that of Davis's version.

FEAR WITHIN THE CITY, FEAR OUTSIDE THE CITY

The response to many of these fears in American cities has been the creation of areas of restricted access where barriers, like those of the early British suburbs, are a physical means to maintain personal safety. This creates different levels of fear in different parts of the city, taking us back to the ideas of Louis Wirth and the creation of anomie, being isolated when attacked. Valentine argues that this isolation is unevenly constructed across the city and, indeed, that it is spatially determined (1992).

EDGE CITY

If the urban planners have failed to recreate the ideal community in the city, and have therefore failed to bring their idealisation of the country into the city, what about taking the city into the country? What about when purely urban values are thrust into the countryside when the effective urban core is transplanted to the outskirts of our towns and cities? Business parks, investments zones and freeports are legion. Housing has followed. The biggest and most dramatic pull from the old central business district to the periphery has been the airport, the multiplex and, of course, the shopping centre. Using the American example, Garreau has provided one of the most compelling analyses of this break in the concentric rings model. He argues that these places contain all the functions that a city ever has, although of course the density is much lower and these functions are spread out over a much greater area.

> *Edge Cities represent the third wave of our lives pushing into new frontiers in this half century. First, we moved our homes out past the traditional idea of what constituted a city. This was the suburbanization of America, especially after the Second World War. Then we wearied of returning downtown for the necessities of life, so we moved our marketplace out to where we lived. This was the malling of America, especially in the 1960s and 1970s. Today we have moved our means of creating wealth, the essence of urbanism – our jobs – out to where most of us have lived and shopped for two generations. This has led to the rise of Edge City.*
>
> *(Garreau, 1998)*

Car ownership, the improvement and expansion of the road network and developments in communication have all made residence outside the city economically much more viable than, it could be argued, at any time since the industrial revolution. Certainly this is the case for our society's high earners and the professional classes.

Study the views of Garreau and work through the following:

- Examine the nearest and/or the most influential shopping centre or retail park near you and write 200 words about it. (The Metro Centre at Gateshead, Newcastle, is one of the largest for example.)
- List the ways in which it has changed the urban experience of those who live and work nearby. Who travels far to use its facilities and why do they do so?
- What is its relationship to the urban core? Think in terms of retailing, transportation, housing, and the location decisions of businesses, especially the large employers in the financial services sector.
- Have such 'edge cities' helped or hindered rural development?

SUMMARY

The argument of this chapter has been twofold. First we have explained how images of the countryside were constructed historically in reaction to fast urban growth. We showed how planners tried to bring the countryside into the city. This approach to the city has been seen as inadequate and hence the second theme of our argument: transplanting the city into the countryside. This breaks the geographical confines of the city and the intellectual confines of the community based on dense familial and friendship networks. The autonomous urban experience of the late twentieth century is no longer just that of a disadvantaged underclass, abandoned in the centre by the flight of the professional classes and those of a higher socio-economic status to the suburbs. The concentric rings model has been complicated by new urban cores being created in the edge of the older urban forms. Edge city has created a new set of urban relationships, a new challenge to notions of community, and has prompted us to a new understanding of the rural–urban continuum. The city has been reasserted over its hinterland.

Group work

The processes of gentrification and revitalisation of old established areas of the city, as well as the earlier processes of suburbanisation and the development of peripheral housing schemes, have all altered spatial relationships within the urban world. They have also had a profound effect on the social relationships that had once been there. The view prevailing today is that the community has been lost, that it has been undermined by structural changes in the topography of the city. In other words our residential choices, the ways in which we choose to live, have cut away the former association and contacts which made a community. How could a sense of community, of collective self-responsibility, be formed, it is argued, in a high-rise on the outskirts of the town or city, where there are no facilities other than a convenience store and an off-licence, and poor transport links? It is the nature of our housing which has caused anomie in the city. How valid is this argument? Divide the class into two: Group A should take a working class housing scheme, Group B a middle class housing estate as their special responsibility. Assess the view that 'it is where we live in the city which makes us the way we are'. Follow this assessment by a full group discussion.

Coursework

Returning to the rural–urban continuum, to what extent do the opposite poles of rural and urban still inform our views, despite attempts at reconciliation by urban planners through developments such as the garden city movement or suburbanisation or 'edge city'? For your evidence, survey a range of children's stories or popular novels. List the key words which the author uses to conjure up images of the rural and urban. Concentrate on how complex ideas are expressed in simple terms, understandable by a child.

Exam Hints

Critically examine the view that de-urbanisation has blurred the distinctions between rural and urban life.

A possible answer to this question would outline the distinctions between rural and urban life, and then make the following points about de-urbanisation: the rejection of urbanisation in the late nineteenth century and of the inner city in the twentieth century; the importance of civil amenities, ecology, gentrification and regeneration of the city; edge city cutting swathes through the greenbelt, refocusing the urban core for both the city and the rural hinterland.

From this chapter, you should now understand the following themes. Take time to make a concept card on each:

- The country in the city: suburbs, model villages, garden cities, small and cathedral towns.
- The city in the country: ecology, gentrification, docklands, urban fear, dangerous areas.
- The role of the country and the 'rural community' in urban planning and in the response to urban decay.
- Edge city.
- Breaking the concentric rings.
- The myth of community.

1   What attempts have been made to analyse the processes of suburbanisation? Evaluate how effective they have been.
2   To what extent does the process of gentrification revitalize a city or undermine its traditional communities?

6

NATIONHOOD AND NATIONAL IDENTITY

Introduction

IN THIS CHAPTER the issue of nationhood and national identity will be examined. These raise questions about 'who we are'. The Mancunian, the Scouser, the Essex man or women, the Highland teuchter, the Cornish man or woman – all conjure up a strong image of regional identities in Britain. Each term encourages what sociologists have called 'labels', short-hand definitions of large groups of people and behaviour based on limited and often incomplete information. What is more, it is argued that the power of the label is such that the very person being labelled starts to believe in it and this encourages more 'characteristic' behaviour. From the comedy of the 1990s, Harry Enfield's 'the Scousers', with permed hair and prominent moustaches, is one good example of the self-fulfilling potential of a label. So far in this book we have stressed the importance of a whole range of different local identities and the link to national identity; no matter the locality or region involved, the Mancunian, the Scouser, the Highlander are all British. They are subjects of the monarch within the United Kingdom of Great Britain and Northern Ireland. They are British and their passport says so.

But this doesn't mean that when these people consider their national identity they think of themselves first and foremost as 'British'. National identity is not as straightforward as that! National identity can be very vague idea and many people use it in quite contradictory ways. In this chapter our aim is to understand just how important national identity has been in the modern world.

Table 9: *Theorists, concepts and issues in this chapter*		
KEY THEORISTS	KEY CONCEPTS	KEY ISSUES
Anderson	Imagined community	Is the national community real?
	'Print capitalism' and vernacular languages	What role for 'communication' in making the nation?
Gellner	Nationality is modern	Why does nationality appear inherent when it is not?
Mazzini	Patria	The national family.
Stalin	Objective/subjective definition of the nation	Can we 'measure' nations and nationality?
Renan	Remembering our past	Explain the 'spiritual essence' of the nation?
Greenfeld	Civic nationalism	Is national identity only about citizenship?
	'Parliament, Crown, Protestantism'	Was England the first nation?
Shils	Citizenship	How easy is it to choose our nationality?
Smith	Ethnic nationalism	Are nations and national identity tied to a community of ethnic descent?
Hobsbawm & Ranger	Invented traditions	How do societies create their history through traditions?
Billig	Banal nationalism	Is our national identity an everyday activity, almost subconscious?
Gellner v Smith	Modern v primordial	Are nations modern?

NATIONALISM AND COMMUNITY

The pulling power of locality and community, it has been shown, lies in their influence on our everyday lives, whether we have a rural, an urban or a 'garden city' mentality. Their immediacy, uncontroversial ordinariness and simplicity is why they have been able to give an identity to a group of individuals who, objectively speaking, are often tied by little more than residence. If this identity is completely absorbed by our social selves, what place is there for national identity?

At a straightforward level, the nation is the community writ large. It is the national community. Yet this simple everyday term, 'national community', requires one of the most amazing transformations in social life to occur – the ability of (usually) geographically defined groups of individuals to think and act in the same way and to claim common cause. This is done at various levels: 'Your country needs you!' is a classic proclamation. But who is telling me this and who or what is my country anyway? Is it the same as your country?

There is an important phrase which lies at the heart of this great collective mind-meld. It comes from Benedict Anderson and is the headline of his most influential book: 'imagined communities'. This term is a useful means towards understanding why national communities exist. An 'imagined' community is not unreal or artificial, a fantasy or a dream. It is no different in terms of people and houses from those communities in the studies of Bethnal or Gosforth or Los Angeles. The power of this term is to highlight how in a national community there can exist a single common set of feelings and emotions. England rugby fans singing 'Swing Low Sweet Chariot' at Twickenham, or the 'national outpouring of grief' which accompanied the sudden death and funeral of Diana, Princess of Wales, are tangible examples. The 'imagined community' is a central concept in the study of nationalism and national identity, and we shall return to it throughout this and the chapters which follow.

The fundamental power of nationalism and the nation-state is that such terms appear to require no definition – that it is obvious what we mean by nation, by a state, by a nation-state, and what we mean by our nationality. For Britain these meanings translate as:

- nation (England, Scotland, Wales, Northern Ireland);
- nationality (English, Scottish, Welsh, Northern Irish, British);
- state (Commons, Lords, Whitehall, monarchy);
- nation-state (The United Kingdom of Great Britain and Northern Ireland).

As students of sociology we should be better able than most to keep such subtleties clear in our analysis; yet it is not unusual for nation, nationality, state and nation-state to be rolled into a straightforward presentation of 'Britain'. We shall soon see that this is a very unsatisfactory shorthand term.

THE NATION AND THE NATION-STATE

The history of the world has become the history of nations – and it is now hard to conceive of anything other than the nation-state being the most important building-block of the modern world order. National boundaries are sacrosanct, each territory has its own state, and violation of that by another is usually regarded as an act of war.

But while the territory may change little over the centuries since the earth was created, the history of how and by whom that territory is governed is incredibly complex. The nation-state has not always existed, yet nationalism as a political movement is virtually always about providing *a* state for *a* people in *a* territory because, it is believed, that was how it once was, and should always be.

A man must have a nationality as he must have a nose and two ears; a deficiency in any of these particulars is not inconceivable and does from time to time occur, but only as the result of some disaster, and it is itself a disaster of its kind. All this seems obvious, though, alas, it is not true. But that it should have come to seem so very obviously true is indeed an aspect, or perhaps the very core, of the problem of nationalism. Having a nation is not an inherent attribute of humanity, but it has now come to appear as such.

(Gellner 1983)

Nationalists appeal to the continuity of the 'past' over generations – and they usually appeal to ethnic or monarchical purity throughout that past. Self-determination is claimed on the grounds that in ancient times a particular people lived on a particular land, and this people were genetically, culturally, and religiously homogeneous. The appeal of nationalism is therefore an appeal to our human emotions – playing on what is vaguely described as 'natural', 'moral', 'right', or a lost 'golden age'. It is about a homeland that is theirs or ours, one that is handed down from generation to generation. This is best understood in the phrase of Guiseppe Mazzini, one of the most influential nineteenth-century nationalist freedom-fighters from Italy. He sums up what we have been saying here in terms of the 'Patria', the national family, which links the generations (Woolf 1996).

Study Point

Contrast the ways in which the public lives of members of the Royal Family can serve to promote or undermine a sense of national identity.

Being the member of a national family, being born into it, living in it, and dying from it, and recognising this to be so, is the Patria – and this sustains nationhood. From this there is a belief in a national division of mankind into nations – that every nation has its own personality or character (sometimes even a mission in the world) which is the product of its history and culture. 'Britannia' or 'John Bull' in Britain, 'Marianne' in France and, in Germany, the 'Great Michael', each is a character which represents the nation to the world. It is believed that all nations have the right to run their own affairs, and only by doing so can a nation reach its full potential. And, especially as the twentieth century developed, the first loyalty of the citizen, of each individual, was and is to the nation-state. Fighting for King and Country means fighting for the nation-state. This is the pulling power of the nation-state as offered by the nationalist:

I against my brother
I and my brother against our cousin
I, my brother and our cousin against the neighbours
All of us against the foreigner

(from Chatwin (1988) *The Songlines*, quoted in Woolf, 1996)

Clearly, then, nationalism is a political movement that taps the most basic primordial or inherent cultural beliefs of a group of people who recognise each other as forming a nation.

WHEN DOES IDENTITY BECOME NATIONAL IDENTITY?

Sociologists, political scientists, historians and anthropologists have all offered guidance on the study of the nation and of nationhood. Yet there remains no single approach, although there have been signs of a convergence to the point of concensus in recent years. There is some agreement on the terms of the debate. First of all, should sociologists use 'objective' or 'subjective' criteria in their research? Examples of objective measurements of the strength of nationalism are language and religion. Mainland Britain has, for most of its history, practised Protestantism as its official religious identity; Ireland and France have been Catholic. This has been taken as an example of how these countries are different nations, and hence why they have often fought each other in the name of nationalism. All three speak or have spoken different languages, and this helps to explain their 'difference'. Other factors that can be counted are population size, industrial development and GDP, although it is generally agreed that such definitions are never sufficient explanations in themselves.

Joseph Stalin, most notable as the dictator of the Soviet Union for 30 years until 1953, offered a series of objective criteria before adding one subjective measurement (Hutchinson and Smith 1994). His five points which identified the nation as a historically constituted stable creation were defined as:

- A common language
- A common territory
- A common economic life
- A common psychological make-up
- A common culture

Study Point
Suggest some reasons why people living on an island, or other area remote from the centre of power in Britain, may not necessarily feel 'British'.

Points of Evaluation
1 These five points, Stalin argued, could explain the demarcating line between nations. His final two indicators, the common psychological make-up manifested through a common culture, are the most relevant, because none of the objective definitions are sufficient in themselves. Religion and language may have separated certain nations as we have seen, but this is not inevitable.

2 English is widely spoken throughout Britain and in the United States of America, but it has not stopped expressions of nationalism between all the nations concerned; nor has Protestantism stopped entirely the rhetoric of opposition between England and Scotland, Wales and Northern Ireland.

3 Subjective criteria tend to be more difficult to define or to compare, but they are often more relevant. What is obtained is a common national psyche, and clearly this is similar to an imagined community. Subjective measurements tend to concentrate on history, on a shared past, where memories of great victories or the actions of warriors or heroes are learned, and so are able to tell people 'who they are'.

Ernest Renen has provided many memorable quotes on the spiritual essence of the nation. Here is just one: 'To have common glories in the past, a common will in the present; to have accomplished great things together, to wish to do so again, that is the essential condition for being a nation.'

In Renan's understanding of the nation we have a geographical locality, where there is a sense of community that goes beyond the people you know and starts to include everyone who you think is part of your nation – that is the power of national identity and of the imagined community. When this spirituality becomes politically active, such as in the SNP or Plaid Cymru or Parti Quebecois, then this national consciousness becomes nationalism. Yet neither national identity nor nationalism is without significance or is possible until a group of individuals is prepared to submerge their local identities to their national identity: to create their own 'imagined community'.

Activity
What is your 'imagined community'?

THE NATION: CIVIC OR ETHNIC?

The heart of the debate in nationalism studies today is this: should the nation be regarded as entirely modern, a creation of the late eighteenth century, or is the nation pre-modern in origin, based on much older loyalties and attachments?

In the academic literature, this debate was most famously stated in 1908 by Friederich Meinecke as follows:

- *Staatsnation* – self-determining political nation
- *Kulturnation* – largely passive cultural nation

More recently Greenfeld has conceptualised this as the 'civic nation' and the 'ethnic nation'. Is a nation defined by its state and/or its demand for a state? Or is a nation defined by its culture, its history, and its ethnicity, whether it has had a state or not? This is a much stronger sense of nationalism than the notion of the *Kulturnation*.

THE CIVIC NATION

The civic nation is a nation that came into being as the modern state developed – it was inevitable, if not functional. One of the clearest expression of the civic nation and the nation-state is the political tie of 'citizenship'. Here the governing of the people is by the legitimate state. Anthony Giddens has proposed that Britain and France were the earliest examples in the West of this uniting of nation and state. This is confirmed by the American sociologist Edward Shils (1995) who has argued that nineteenth-century intellectuals in England and France were aware that the Glorious Revolution of 1689, and the 1789 French Revolution, imposed a state on a nation in return for the extension of 'citizenship rights'. By so doing, Giddens argues, it legitimated the state and its control over internal and external violence (ie the police and the armed forces).

Indeed, Greenfeld has gone back further in history to suggest that this process has taken place in England since the sixteenth century:

At a certain point in history – to be precise early sixteenth-century England – the word 'nation' in its conciliar meaning of 'an elite' was applied to the population of the country and made synonymous with the word 'people'. This semantic transformation signalled the emergence of the first nation in the world, in the sense in which the word is understood today, and launched the era of nationalism ...

(Greenfield 1992)

Study Point
Would you favour more lessons in schools on citizenship? Or is this a form of indoctrination?

In this particular account of the nation, as exemplified in the definition of Edward Shils, 'nationality' is closest to 'citizenship' in the nation-state. In the literature this is termed a 'Western model' of the nation and it is tied in fundamentally with the idea of the state: it is the nation-state which makes the nation, and the nation could not exist otherwise. This is a very open model. In fact, in this model of nationality, you could choose your nation. As individuals we can change our nationality by changing our 'nation of residence'. Greg Rusedski and Martina Navratilova are recent examples in the tennis world of individuals who, on reaching adulthood, have changed their nationality.

So in these terms nationality is open. It can be defined either by:

- birth in a specifically bounded territory, or
- residence in that bounded territory, or
- descent from persons resident in that bounded territory.

If we take the most extreme expression of the civic nation and civic nationality, it is the 'United States of the World', where loyalty is to the world, not to the nation (Greenfeld 1992).

Points of Evaluation

1 One implication of this 'Western model' is that we can have similar nationalities at the same time (eg English or Scottish or Iranian or Pakistani and British).
2 Another is that the state can choose to use all or only one of these categories in accepting citizenship.
3 The history of the postwar Immigration Acts and the granting (or not) of British citizenship to those born in British colonies (and ex-colonies) is indicative of how racism can distort this civic definition.
4 But biology and race are generally absent from this model; here the nation and nationality are features of the state – of politics.
5 To extend this definition, the most open version of the civic model, argues Shils, meant that citizenship and nationality came to mean the same thing. This occurred because a new kind of policy – the rational state – and a new kind of community – the territorial nation – first appeared in the West at roughly the same time.
6 With the break up of empires and the shift from absolutism to rational states by the eighteenth century, the single, territorial state came into existence.

Activity
Undertake a short study by sampling a group to discover their conception of 'nationality' (birth place; residence; descent). Does this vary between age, gender, class or ethnicity?

THE ETHNIC NATION

Despite linking the nation and national identity to the state and citizenship, a central part of any nation is how it is *imagined*. That is, it is fundamentally a function of collective self-consciousness: a state of mind reflecting on a collective 'past'. Hence a different conception of the nation is the ethnic nation.

In contrast to the ideas discussed in the last section, an 'ethnic' conception of the nation is a non-Western model. Its distinguishing feature is its emphasis on a community of birth and native culture. By far the leading proponent of this view, and critic of the modernists, is Anthony D. Smith. He argues that unlike, say, the example of the two tennis players Navratilova and Rusedski, whether you stay in a nation or leave for another nation you never lose your attachment to the community of your birth. In other words, a nation is first and foremost a 'community of common descent' (Smith 1991).

The primary criterion of membership is birth or prolonged residence in the bounded territory by a people with a deep level of self-awareness. That is what is referred to as national collective self-consciousness. In this ethnic model the role taken by law in the Western civic model is replaced by vernacular culture, such as everyday spoken languages and particular customs.

Genealogy and presumed descent ties, popular mobilisation, vernacular languages, customs and traditions: these are the elements of an alternative, ethnic conception of the nation, one that mirrored the very different route of 'nation-formation' travelled by many communities in Eastern Europe and Asia and one that constituted a dynamic political challenge ... it reflects a profound dualism at the heart of every nationalism.

(Smith 1991)

In a more explicit way than the modernists', this is a theory which incorporates race. Yet it does so at a cultural not a biological level. Thus, when neighbouring groups look alike physically, such as Anglo-Saxons and Celts, then cultural markers are more effective than genetics for assessing national group membership.

MIXTURE OF THE CIVIC AND THE ETHNIC NATION

Smith believes that nationalism as a world force is indeed modern, but even so, he maintains, national identity remains rooted in older ethnic ties. In fact, argues Smith, every nationalism contains civic and ethnic elements in varying degrees and different forms:

- A historic territory and homeland
- Common myths and historical memories
- A common, mass public culture
- Common legal rights and duties for all members
- A common economy with territorial mobility for members

A nation is therefore defined by Smith 'as a named human population sharing an historic territory, common myths and historical memories, a mass, public culture, a common economy and common legal rights and duties for all members.' For Smith the nation is a political creation where the past and present exist simultaneously. Clearly 'descent' is important in nationhood and there is a tendency for residence or territoriality to turn, in the mind, into 'blood' or at least 'blood-like' physical features, fostering close links.

We therefore do not have a complete compromise between the two models because Smith and his colleagues reject the outright civic modern (especially the statist model proposed by Anthony Giddens). The link between ethnicity and citizenship is territory. Yet this is flexible, and so national identity is far from being about biological descent.

THE 'INVENTION OF TRADITION'

The disagreement between the modernists – those who support the civic nation – and the ethno-symbolists or primordialists – those who favour the ethnic nation – comes down to the extent to which national identity is forged on a historical past or 'golden age' of a historical people (race) or to which it only *seems old* but is in fact modern. The later position is argued by Gellner and Anderson as we have seen, and also by E.J. Hobsbawm. With his colleague Terence Ranger, Hobsbawm has offered one of the most powerful analyses of how nation-states go about creating a national past. This is the idea of the 'invented tradition'. It is regarded by many as one of the key techniques states and monarchies use to engender loyalty from citizens or subjects.

Invented tradition is taken to mean a set of practices, normally governed by overtly or tacitly accepted rules and of a ritual or symbolic nature, which seek to inculcate certain values and norms of behaviour by repetition, which automatically implies continuity with the past. In fact, where possible, they normally attempt to establish continuity with a suitable historical past.

(Hobsbawm and Ranger, (1994) *The Invention of Tradition*, Canto)

Hobsbawm sets out three types of invented tradition:

- Those establishing or symbolising social cohesion or the membership of groups, real or artificial communities.
- Those establishing or legitimising institutions, status relations of authority.
- Those whose main purpose was socialisation, the inculcation of beliefs, values systems and conventions of behaviour.

One of the best sets of examples, he argues, is the flag, the anthem and the emblem: 'The National Flag, the National Anthem, and the National Emblem are the three symbols through which an independent country proclaims its identity and sovereignty, and as such they command instantaneous respect and loyalty. In themselves they reflect the entire background, thought and culture of a nation.'

The flag and the national anthem are good examples too of the construction of what Michael Billig has called 'banal nationalism' (Billig 1995). This is the nationalism of the everyday, the waving of the flag or the painting of the parts of the town to be seen during a royal visit. It is singing the national anthem at the award of a gold medal at the Olympics or before an international football match. This is at the opposite end of the scale from genocide or ethnic cleansing which is often taken to be the logical conclusion of nationalism. The banality of nationalism, based on a series of interlinked invented traditions, is equally valid and by far the more common experience of nationalism in the world today.

Activity

Use the idea of the 'invented tradition' as your conceptual tool and write 50–100 words on just why any one of the examples below is not as old as it seems. In what ways are any of these examples part of the state-promotion or national identity?

- Monuments to Robin Hood or William Wallace or any other hero.
- The Union Jack flag and the British National Anthem.
- The Cenotaph and the Tomb of the Unknown Soldier.
- The Investiture of the Prince of Wales, 1969.
- The State Opening of Parliament.

IS THE NATION MODERN?

In the journal *Nations and Nationalism*, Volume 2, Part 3 (1996) Ernest Gellner debated whether the nation and the nation-state was modern or not. The debate was with his former student Anthony D. Smith.

At its heart, the disagreement concerns whether nations and nation-states were wholly created in the period since about the eighteenth century, with the French Revolution in 1789 being a particular landmark. It as argued that as the old European associations of countries, such as the Holy Roman and Habsburg empires were breaking up, they were replaced by powerful monarchs who ruled over geographically limited nations. In turn, these monarchs were replaced by liberal states of varying constitutional openness. This final period of change, in and around eighteenth century, was, it is argued by modernists, when the nation-state was formed. For these states to be legitimate there was a process of tying the people to the state through notions of citizenship – this was the prime mechanism for engendering loyalty to the state from the people. The state had to make the link between the people and itself and this it did through creating a sense of solidarity, by inventing traditions. Now, could these states make and create loyalty as they pleased? Could the state make a nation-state where there was no ethnic basis to the nation? This is the central question being debated.

To explore this debate, we start with Smith's critique of the modernist position which is summarised below:

- The generality of the modernist's argument – 'Though they make out a convincing case for explaining 'nationalism-in-general', they are often pitched at such a level of abstraction that they cannot be easily applied to specific areas or cases.'
- 'Nationalism can emerge in all kinds of socio-economic milieu – in rich Quebec and poor Eritrea, in areas of decline as well as improvements, in pre-industrial as well as industrial conditions.'
- The most critical problem, Smith argues, is their commitment to the idea that nations and nationalism are products of modernisation. 'What this systematically overlooks is the persistence of ethnic ties and cultural sentiments in many parts of the world, and their continuing significance to large numbers of people.'

Study Point

Suggest three factors that turn a small group of people living together into a small nation.

The response from Gellner was to ask if nations, like Adam, have navels or not? His metaphor is a powerful one. If Adam didn't have a navel, then he was created by God, and was therefore not born of woman. Adam could have been created out of nothing and so could the state – it did not need to be born of a prior ethnic identity. Yet, he goes on to argue, does it matter anyway? Ethnic identity is important for some nations, but not for many others.

> My main case for modernism that I'm trying to highlight in this debate, is that on the whole the ethnic, the cultural national community, which is such an important part of Anthony's [Smith] case, is rather like the navel. Some nations have it and some don't and in any case it's inessential.
>
> … There are very, very clear cases of modernism in a sense being true. I mean, take the Estonians. At the beginning of the nineteenth century they didn't even have a name for themselves. They were just referred to as people who lived on the land as opposed to German and Swedish burghers, aristocrats and Russian administrators. They had no ethnonym. They were just a category without any ethnic self-consciousness.
>
> … So I would say in general that there is a certain amount of navel about but not everywhere and on the whole it's not important.

(Gellner, 1996)

SUMMARY

National identity is a complex issue. There are many pressures on people to make them feel a member of a particular nation, through the use of symbols and calls to patriotic support, especially in times of crisis or when representatives are competing in some way against others. National boundaries are established and become sacred, defended at all costs. This sense of identity can lead to all kinds of problems; non-members are identified and often become the subject of jokes or negative stereotyping. No single way of answering the question – what is a nation and how should nationhood be understood and analysed? – has been achieved. Some defining qualities have been suggested, relating to shared language and culture, territory and economy, so that we may develop a concept of our 'imagined community'. Confusions arise because some people seem to share different nationalities and allegiances. Debates have developed between sociologists to try to identify the various strands which distinguish civic from ethnic nationalism. Some see it as a political creation and others as something inherent and unique. In their attempt to instil a sense of national identity, some leaders have invented traditions to give a sense of history and made use of symbols like flags and ceremonies. Critics have argued that ethnic identity is valued by some nations and some individuals but not by others.

STUDY GUIDE

Group work

Whether or not nations and nation-states are more ethnic or more civic in their foundations, we have stressed that the power of national identity is the very simplicity of the message. Unfortunately, many of the sociological theories offered to help understand this phenomenon are rather complex and need a little thought to work through. With someone else, or in a group, choose a selection of the following quotes and try to interpret them. What do the authors mean and how do their statements help us understand nationalism? Try to get these texts if you can so that you can place the quotes in their proper context. If not, the information contained in the sections you have read for this chapter will give you many clues. But don't do all the work on your own: discussing these quotes in a group is the best approach.

Ernest Gellner

Gellner argues that the modern nation-state was the most efficient means to develop international capitalism.

Nationalism is a theory of political legitimacy which requires that ethnic boundaries should not cut across political ones, and, in particular, that ethnic boundaries within a given state … should not separate the power holders from the rest.

… a society has emerged based on a high-powered technology and the expectancy of sustained growth, which requires both a mobile division of labour and sustained, frequent and precise communication between strangers involving a sharing of explicit meaning, transmitted in a standard idiom and in writing when required.

(Gellner 1983)

Benedict Anderson

The impact of this standard idiom for commerce was also at the heart of the bringing together of the national 'imagined community'. The rise of the printing press, reproducing the spoken languages, not Latin and not only for the most highly educated, began the promotion and cohesion of one common thought-world. The newspaper, the poster, the popular novel, as well as the reporting of parliament, tied 'the people' to each other and to the state in a way that had never been achieved before. This common national understanding was essential to forming the 'imagined community' which was the nation: 'the convergence of capitalism and print technology on the fatal diversity of human language created the possibility of a new form of community, which in its basic morphology set the stage for the modern nation' (1991).

Anthony D. Smith

Yet we must conclude with Smith and his insistence that even older identities, pre-dating enfranchised politics (citizenship) and print-capitalism, have nearly always played an essential role in nation and nation-state formation.

He has accepted that nations are modern phenomena in so far as they:

- are legally unified with the existence of citizenship rights;
- are based on a single economy;
- have a compact territory which is easily defensible; and
- require a single 'political culture' to socialise 'citizens' of the future

while continuing to insist that:

Ethnic distinctiveness remains a sine que non *of the nation, and that means shared ancestry myths, common historical memories, unique cultural markers, and a sense of difference, if not election – all the elements that marked off ethnic communities in pre-modern eras. In the modern nation they must be preserved, indeed cultivated, if the nation is not to become invisible.*

(Smith 1991)

Coursework

In her book *Nationalism: Five Roads to Modernity* (Harvard University Press, 1992) Leah Greenfeld has argued that England was the first nation in the world. As we have seen already in this chapter, she argued that in England the idea of the 'nation' was the first to encompass both the elites and the common people in a single common agenda. Greenfeld took as her evidence the solution to conflict around monarchical power and England's religious faith as her dominant themes, an argument echoed by Edward Shils. Greenfeld develops her thesis by pointing out how England solved the conflict which existed between the crown and the state in favour of the latter, and established a state religion (Protestantism) which its people agreed to. In both cases, it had achieved stability and coherence well before the age of nationalism in the 1790s and 1840s. This, she and others have argued, is the key to why England/Britain has not been subject to the extreme forms of political turmoil which were witnessed elsewhere in Europe, historically and today.

Your task is to analyse the history and religion of the monarchy in England/Britain, concentrating on either of these two themes:

- Its relationship to the Houses of Parliament.
- Its influence and impact on the lives of the people of England.

You will need to do some further reading and research on the monarchy in Britain. Perhaps start at the official home page of the British monarchy, maintained by the government: http://www.royal.gov.uk/. Look at the work of

David Cannadine (1983) and Tom Nairn (1988). Contrast these with any of the popular 'coffee-table' accounts of the royal family which have appeared in recent years.

Exam Hints

How have sociologists attempted to explain the changes in nationalism and national identity in contemporary societies?

This question relates to the central concerns of this chapter. A possible answer would focus on the following points: identifying the nation by objective and subjective criteria; civic versus ethnic nationalism; modern nationalism – the role of the state; the influence of primordial memories/ethnic symbolism; the invention of tradition. You will also need to discuss the changes in the types of nationalism and in national identity which have occurred in recent years.

Revision Hints

From this chapter, you should now understand the following themes. Take time to make a key concept card on each:

- The conflation between nation, nationality, state and nation-state.
- The assumed 'naturalness' of the nation-state.
- Objective and subjective criteria in determining the transition from personal identity to national identity.
- Civic/ethnic nationalism.
- Modern/primordial (ethno-symbolist) nationalism.
- The invention of traditional banal nationalism versus ethnic cleansing.
- The key definitions.

Practice Questions

1 What light have sociologists thrown on the study of the nation and of nationhood?
2 Critically examine the views that 'Nationalism is a political ideology; and nationalists appeal to the continuity of the past over generations'.

7

ONE STATE, MANY NATIONS

Introduction

IN THIS CHAPTER we explore why it seems straightforward to regard Great Britain as a leading European example of the stable nation-state, one that has remained free from nationalism. This perception of coherent nation-statehood has masked conflict within British national identity. To claim to be British is to claim neutrality or nothingness and it denies loyalty to whichever of the four nations was the place of one's birth. To be 'British' is today increasingly anachronistic. This claim to be British is, for many unproblematically, the wider identity of those who are English. Yet we must be aware of the social processes in Britain and in the world more generally which increasingly undermine such confidence in the term 'British'. The issue of race and of ethnic and other minorities is a further challenge to notions of national coherence and of citizenship. Is the British identity, then, just ignoring more fundamental local or national identities?

Table 10: *Theorists, concepts and issues in this chapter*		
KEY THEORISTS	KEY CONCEPTS	KEY ISSUES
Morton	British 'nation-state'	Why is this too broad a conception?
	Civil society	The Westminster state and four civil societies.
Kohn	English national consciousness	Why was English nationalism said not to exist?
Taylor	Crown heartland	What role has the monarchy in Englishness?
Gilroy	National boundaries	Are the theories of national identity in Britain blind to race?

Cashmore	Race and community 'New racism'	The fears that Britain was to lose its 'way of life' following Commonwealth immigration.
Tebbit	Multi-culturalism	How valid is the 'cricket test'?
Jacobson	Britishness	How do ethnic minorities become accepted as being 'British'?
	A declaration for the North	Is Britain to break up following Scottish and Welsh devolution?

THE BRITISH 'NATION-STATE'?

While there is some community of interest called Britain and common institutions and historical experiences called British, and indeed a nationality on a passport called British, it is not an identity which is self-contained ... Britain is a state rather than a nation. The British state imposed upon the English, Scottish, Welsh and part of the Irish peoples and then imposed world wide, is an inherently imperial and colonial concept at home and abroad. The British state cannot and should not be an object of affection, save for those who want to live in a form of authoritarian dependency.

(Dafydd Elis Thomas, quoted in Gilroy 1996)

It is interesting that this quote by the former Leader of Plaid Cymru, Dafydd Elis Thomas, should be reproduced by an author studying race in Britain today, because its main concern was to highlight the conflict between the peripheral nations of Scotland, Wales and Northern Ireland with conceptions of Britishness. The conflict between core and periphery and the success (or otherwise) of multiculturalism in Britain are the themes of this chapter, the reason being that they are undermining confidence in the British 'nation-state'.

WHO ARE THE BRITISH ANYWAY?

As sociologists we must ask if it is analytically relevant to use the term 'British'? There is still no agreed colloquial name for the United Kingdom: 'Britain', 'Great Britain', the 'Brits'? The formal position is as stated by Kellas (1984):

- United Kingdom (UK) – United Kingdom of Great Britain and Northern Ireland
- Britain – short version of the above
- Great Britain (GB) – England, Wales and Scotland

DUAL IDENTITIES: ONE STATE, FOUR CIVIL SOCIETIES

The British nation-state, then, is too inaccurate a conception. A more productive concept for getting at the heart of the national divisions within the United

Kingdom is 'civil society'. When we talk of the four nations and their single state, theorists often use the term 'civil society'. It is useful shorthand for the arena where different cultures and institutions can exist within the one political system.

> *At its most straightforward, civil society is the social structure which exists between the household and the state and it is an arena where extensive and intricate association can take place without personal obligation. What obligation there is, comes from a sense of civic virtue.*
>
> *(Morton 1998a)*

The distinct civil societies within the British state have produced 'dual nationalities' – where its nationals can be British if they wish or, if not, they can 'opt out' and their identity can return to being a Welsh, a Northern Irish, an English or a Scottish one. These citizens of the United Kingdom are entitled to dual or even multiple identities (when religion or language are introduced). All this contributes to stressing how false is the conceptualisation of Great Britain as a single 'nation-state'. To emphasise this, Raymond Williams has christened the UK as 'Yookay'; for Tom Nairn it is 'Ukania'. Each of these nicknames is intended to highlight the ambiguity within the supposed classical British nation-state (Morton 1998b).

Study Point

How might we maintain dual national identities in the United Kingdom? List five examples of your national and your British identity.

THE BEGINNINGS OF ENGLISH NATIONAL IDENTITY

ENGLAND AS ISLAND, AND THE FREE-BORN IDENTITY

Conventionally, England is identified as an island despite being only part of one. The defeat of the Spanish Armada in 1588 is the most likely peg upon which this belief hangs. Shakespeare's evocation of the 'scept'red isle' is one of the more enduring symbols of English identity – loyalty to royalty and the island. At the time of the Reformation, what better justification could there be for the break with Rome than that of ancient British traditions of independence – physically separate, therefore religiously separate, and also legally free (Evans 1989). The claims of Parliament after the 'Glorious Revolution' of 1688 rested essentially on the idea of an ancient constitution enshrined in Magna Carta and the Bill of Rights as well as more generally in Common Law. In this version of history, opposition to the threat of invasion is mobilised around the powerful notion of the 'free-born Englishman' and freedom from the 'Norman Yoke'.

Kohn's study of nationalism (1946) was the first to declare that the English nation was born in the Puritan and confirmed in the Glorious Revolution, and so lost its problematic character. The outcome of these revolutions was:

- the supremacy of the law over the king;
- the supremacy of Parliament in law-making;
- the impartiality of justice;
- the security of individual rights;
- the freedom of thought and press;
- religious tolerance.

ENGLISH NATIONALISM?

Instead of a literature of nationalism the English developed a literature of imperialism. For example, many of Rudyard Kipling's imperial stories contained a stereotype from each of the nations which denied hostility to the others:

- An English officer, a little slow and rigid, but decent.
- A Scottish engineer, dour, but resourceful.
- A Welsh NCO, cunning but dependable.
- An Irish squaddie, coarse, comic, but courageous (Crick 1989).

Study Point

Explain the meaning of 'stereotypes'. Suggest why they are used and why they are dangerous.

The myth of the 'absence of nationalism' is of great importance. Nationalism is seen as something that is 'foreign' to England: patriotism takes the place of nationalism. Patriotism means the love of one's country, nationalism means power to the people. Patriotism means loyalty to the current social or political order; nationalism carries the threat of revolution.

Yet a sense of Englishness prevails. The Queen's English is a 'badge of honour' – against which regional dialects are inferior pronunciation. The result is a social world maintained through the education system where the public schools such as Eton, Harrow and Rugby, plus the universities of Oxford and Cambridge dominate. In this version of the Patria it is the Home Counties which predominate – not the homeland. There we find prestigious sports events at Henley, Ascot, Wimbledon, and the Oxford versus Cambridge University Boat Race.

Lords, Twickenham and Wembley, Windsor Castle and Buckingham Palace are there too. This really is a 'Royal heartland' (Taylor 1991). Linked to it is the power of the rural idyll, the rural England of the south – the rolling downs – not the northern wilds of the Yorkshire Moors.

To capture the essence of the English/Britain character we can turn to Prime Minster Harold Macmillan's description of the spirit of D-Day in 1945.

Even the humblest could feel that they were taking part in the making of history. As the new Armada was being prepared against us, we seemed indeed the heirs of Queen Elizabeth and her captains. All the great figures of the past – Drake, Raleigh, Marlborough, Chatham, Wolfe, Pitt, Nelson, Wellington – seemed again alive and almost standing at our side. The unity of the nation was complete and unshakeable.

(Quoted in Osmond 1988)

It is the monarchy that has played a major role in ensuring stability and acting as a prime focus for British identity. Take, for instance, the Queen's 60th birthday celebrations in 1986 when the media took the occasion to plug the Queen's biography into key moments of national history, especially those of the Second World War. The two princesses (Elizabeth and Margaret) on *Children's Hour*, encouraging and giving solace to evacuees in their plight, is a prime example (Nairn 1988).

Points of Evaluation

1   The power of this identity comes from merging of the rural idyll with notions of royalty and 'middle England' which impacts on the world through the spread of liberal democracy and military might.

2   Indeed, to a large extent English/British nationalism is carried by military, and particularly naval prowess legitimated by royal authority (Colley 1992).

3   Perhaps the annual event that best symbolises the military, royal and parliamentary projection of Britain as *one* nation is the Remembrance Day ceremony at London's Cenotaph with its military march-past, the royal laying of a wreath, and the presence of the leaders of the parliamentary parties, including those from Wales, Scotland and Northern Ireland.

Activity
Suggest some of the functional alternatives in periods of peace by which young people can express their sense of nationalism when they cannot express their patriotism through war.

MAKING BRITISH IDENTITY

NORTHERN IRELAND

The biggest challenge to 'Britishness', the rule of law and the territorial integrity of the United Kingdom, has come from over the Irish Channel. The conflict between mainland Britain and Ireland is one with a long history. Its modern form can be traced back to the plantation towns of the fifteenth and sixteenth centuries.

- The Catholic/nationalist myth concerns their land being taken over by English and Scottish farmers setting up plantation towns – where the rights of Irish tenant farmers were removed.
- The Protestant myth is the Battle of the Boyne, the 12th of July, and the Siege of Derry with the slogan of 'No Surrender'.

The land issue has been politicised ever since the plantations and the Penal Laws of 1695 which restricted Catholic land-ownership. They still inform political debate over the future of Northern Ireland, as does its nationalist history:

- The **Orange Order** takes its name from King William of Orange who defeated the Catholic James VII and II at the Battle of the Boyne in 1690. Their original oath enjoined members 'to support the King and his heirs as long as he or they support the Protestant Ascendancy'.
- The formation of **Young Ireland** in the 1840s: the *Nation* newspaper gained a readership of around 250,000 at its peak in 1843.
- In 1858 **Fenianism** was formally constituted as the **Irish Republican Brotherhood** (or the Irish Revolutionary Brotherhood, IRB), partly out of the anti-English sections of Young Ireland. It was supported strongly in the United States. The name 'Fenians' was taken from the legendary warrior order of pre-Christian Ireland.
- **Clan na Gael** was a counter-reaction to this, and it started the movements towards full independence.
- The politician **Charles Stewart Parnell** represented a compromise between the flagrant imperialism of Isaac Butt and the anti-English expressions of Patrick Ford (of Clan na Gael) and the American Fenians.
- Between the 1880s and 1921 British governments made successive attempts to solve the Irish problem by some form of Home Rule. The **partition of Ireland** created the Irish Free State on 1 January 1922.
- The **Irish Republican Army** (IRA) was formed by Michael Collins following the Easter Rising of 1916.
- **Sinn Fein** was founded in 1902 by Arthur Griffith; in 1938 it became the political arm of the IRA.
- **British troops** were first stationed in Northern Ireland in 1969.
- The **Anglo-Irish Agreement** of 1985 was to foster cooperation between Britain and Ireland on security and government in the North.

- The **Downing Street Declaration** (1993) was the British government's wish to enable 'the people of Ireland to reach an agreement on how they may live together in harmony'.
- In 1998, cross-party agreement on a **Northern Ireland Assembly** was reached, allowing also for power sharing institutions linking North and South. In addition, it was agreed that a change to the Republic's constitution would be made, accepting that Northern Ireland will remain part of the UK for as long as the majority desire it.

Activity

Consider whether Northern Ireland should remain part of the United Kingdom or should join a united Ireland. Take the historical evidence and the views expressed in the Social Attitudes Survey in Table 11 as your starting point.

- In the light of your conclusions, what are the implications for the 'peace process' today?
- Write to INCORE at the University of Ulster (or consult their www page: http://www.incore.ulst.ac.uk/) to get further information for your studies.

Table 10: *Views on the status of Northern Ireland within the United Kingdom*

| | Britain | | | Northern Ireland | | |
	1989	1990	1991	1989	1990	1991
Percentage saying that:						
There should be a united Ireland	55	56	54	24	25	22
British troops should be withdrawn	59	60	58	32	32	25

Table 11: *Views on the status of Northern Ireland among Protestants and Catholics*

	Protestant	Catholic
Percentage in Northern Ireland saying that:		
There should be a united Ireland	4	53
The Union should be maintained	92	35
British troops should be withdrawn	11	49
British troops should *not* be withdrawn	86	38

Source: British Social Attitudes Survey, 9th Report (1992/3)

WALES: A FUSED IDENTITY

Welsh nationalism has always been very strong as a cultural idea, but rather weak politically. In contrast to both Scotland and Northern Ireland, Wales does not have a strong institutional basis to its civil society. As a result of its literary renaissance of the eighteenth century, Welsh life was steeped in folklore and poetry. Yet at the start of the twentieth century, Wales gathered some elements of an institutional civil society (although it had to wait until 1963 for a Welsh Secretary):

- At the end of 1893 the University of Wales received the royal assent.
- In 1905 a National Library of Wales was sanctioned.
- In 1907 the Welsh Department set up the Ministry of Education.

In the 1880s there were many influential Welsh-language chapels to serve as assemblies for the people. The Welsh language remained securely based in terms of daily intercourse, far more so than the languages of Ireland and Scotland. Welsh was the language of contemporary argument and discussion (and this was very important to its vibrancy), until it was slowly undermined by the poverty of the nation and its need to industrialise on the coat-tails of England. In the decade 1901-11, the Welsh coalfields attracted 129,000 workers, mainly from England and speaking English. Yet we must not ignore the fact that a major factor in the decline of Welsh speaking was political, not just economic: the government actively discouraged Welsh speaking at this time. The strongest example is banning the speaking of Welsh in the classroom. This played a large part in the denigration of the Welsh language, and also in the actual number of Welsh speakers.

In the early to mid nineteenth century, side-by-side with the growth of industry came the equally explosive growth of religious nonconformity, through the Methodists, Independents and Baptists. The Religious Census of 1851 showed that 80 per cent of Welsh men and women who worshipped went to nonconformist chapels. The cultural and educational resources were there to sustain a Welsh national identity throughout the twentieth century, but to turn such national consciousness into nationalism in its fullest sense a political aspect was also necessary – but this was missing. Welsh radicals were essentially British liberals rather than Celtic nationalists. The emergence of the Welsh national party Plaid Cymru in 1925 took the premise that Welsh culture was preserved in rural society. This creed was especially hostile to the industrial society of the south and cosmopolitan popular culture which inhabited it. South Wales was linked by its trade unionism into the structure of Britain, and very conscious of itself as an industrial society. It saw the rest of Wales as undeveloped.

> ### Study Point
>
> - How might Welsh people who are living in other areas of the country express their Welshness at various times of the year?
> - Why might only a small proportion of these people who identify with Wales declare themselves to be nationalists?

Economics, Language and Devolution

The Depression of the 1920s and 1930s hit a Welsh industry based too narrowly on the primary production of coal and steel, and this was further damaged once foreign markets had been lost. Welsh unemployment reached 38 per cent in 1932 with the result that much out-migration followed. By 1940 Wales was far more socially divided than it had been in 1900. Wales then became very pro-Labour. Plaid Cymru remained a small movement, largely University and rurally orientated and based on a declining constituency of Welsh speakers. But language was again to come to the fore as the main support of cultural nationalism. BBC (Wales) was started in February 1964 and the Welsh language became political dynamite – the Welsh Language Movement gained partial credit for such triumphs as the Welsh Language Act of 1967 giving Welsh validity with English, and it achieved a far more sensitive response from government departments than had been received before. With the Kilbrandon Report of October 1973, devolution for Wales (and Scotland) became for the first time since the 1980s a serious issue.

The Welsh Assembly proposed at the time was to have executive powers instead of the legislative role of the proposed Scottish assembly. Yet Welshness and Welsh politics became secondary when British interests were at stake, and there was a heavy 4 to 1 vote against the idea of an Assembly in the ensuing referendum. The crucial vote of 1979 was followed by a huge swing to the Tories in the General Election which followed in that year.

Wales has not had the institutions that Scotland has had – hence the strength of regional identities and the problems in forging a Welsh citizenship. The establishment of a Welsh fourth television channel, S4C, which came into being in 1982 helped sustain a sense of Welshness. Culturally, too, the 1981 Census saw a slight increase in the number of schoolchildren speaking Welsh, with around 6000 adults learning Welsh at night school. Since the late 1980s, it has become compulsory for all public signs and government literature to be bilingual in Wales; there have also been many more Welsh schools set up and Welsh streams in English speaking schools. A greater political confidence in Welsh national identity witnessed success for devolution in the 1997 referendum, but the narrowness of the victory, 50.1 per cent in favour with 49.9 per cent against, suggests that a strong identification with Britishness remains.

SCOTLAND: MORE CIVIL SOCIETY, LESS COMMUNITY

Arguably the sense of local community in Scotland has been weaker than its sense of Scottish national community (although there are important exceptions such as Shetland and Orkney and perhaps even in Glasgow). Ironically this was probably the reason behind its strength. Scotland has maintained a strong civil society, that area of social structure between the family and the state. Most famously, Scotland has since 1707 and the Union of Parliament with England, structured its national identity around its religion, its legal system and its education system. Kirk, law and education were guaranteed as separate from their English counterparts in the Union settlement, and have remained more than just cultural icons. Today this institutional difference translates into the maintenance of the Presbyterian variant of Protestantism, with no bishops and 'much less colour'; a separate and unique legal jurisdiction based on Roman law, not common law, with its own particular features such as the verdict 'not proven'; plus an education system based on a wide and more general curriculum epitomised at university level with the four-year general degree.

Although the sense of a Scottish national community has probably been stronger than the sense of a local community, there was a feeling that Scotland as a whole needed different political solutions to those of its southern neighbour. In the 1920s and 1930s this view emerged as 'corporate bias', a means of government intervention with public money into the economy. Government quangos were set up to coordinate this intervention such as the Scottish National Development Council (1931) and the Scottish Economic Committee (1936).

Study Point
Suggest some reasons to explain why the sense of local community in Scotland is relatively weak, whilst the sense of identification with Scotland is quite strong.

Politics and devolution
In the years following the Second World War, Labour presented itself as the party of centralism which would use the welfare state to iron out personal as well as regional inequalities. This explains why it dropped its demands for Home Rule. As Britain became a more secular society and the post-imperial state contracted abroad but expanded at home, so its 'national' identity became more problematic. The solution to this was to construct a new sense of Britishness out of the postwar welfare state – this had to be done in Scotland in the face of a new politics of Scottish nationalism.

The Scottish National Party (SNP) came to political prominence in 1967 when Winnie Ewing won a by-election in Hamilton from Labour, but there had been signs of the nationalists doing well since the 1950s when they had been consistently getting around 10 per cent of the vote at by-elections. At the October 1974 election the SNP took 30 per cent of the vote – their highest share at a general election to date. They did proportionately well among all social classes, but particularly amongst those who were socially and geographically mobile members of the lower middle and working classes. Its recruitment was strongest amongst those living in the recently established and growing New Towns such as East Kilbride, Irvine, Livingston and Glenrothes.

Mirroring this political change was a separate Scottish cultural and political agenda established through the media in the 1950s and 1960s. Scottish issues were then seen as separate from those of the United Kingdom. Because the SNP was effectively free from the electoral heartlands which sustained the Labour and the Conservative parties, it could capture the 'Scottish agenda' very easily. By the 1970s, this was reinforced by the discovery of North Sea Oil and the cry of 'It's Scotland's Oil!'. This once again took Scotland's politics to a heightened sense of separateness from that of the United Kingdom, yet in response Scots heard the cry 'It's Shetland's Oil!', emphasising the continued importance of local attachments.

The SNP vote was reduced in 1979. This rejection followed the devolution vote of a few months earlier when, although over half (51.6 per cent) of those who went to the ballot box voted for devolution, 48.4 per cent said no. The turnout was 62.9 per cent and not enough to overcome Cunningham's 40 per cent rule which made it a requirement that at least that number of the whole electorate (not just those who voted) should be in favour (non votes counted as 'no' votes).

The Thatcher government's reforms of the welfare state and of corporatism in the late 1980s were less readily accepted in Scotland than in other parts of the United Kingdom. The levying of the Poll Tax in Scotland a year before the rest of the United Kingdom, it was argued, contradicted the Union of 1707 (which excluded taxes being imposed on Scotland and not on England). In September 1997, exactly 700 years to the date after the Scottish patriot William Wallace defeated the English at the Battle of Stirling Bridge, Scotland voted for a developed parliament with tax-raising powers, and with the Secretary of State for Scotland losing his or her full status in the British Cabinet and a reduction of Scottish MPs at Westminster.

Activity
In what ways can it be argued that dual and even multiple national identities exist in the United Kingdom? To start with, look at Table 12. It shows different levels of allegiance to the idea of 'Britishness' throughout the United Kingdom. How do you explain these differences?

Table 12: *Identity in Britain (data for 1993/4)*			
	ENGLAND %	SCOTLAND %	WALES %
Think of self as:			
'X' not British	16	37	28
More 'X' than British	12	27	20
Equally 'X' and British	43	25	30
More British than 'X'	10	4	7
British, not 'X'	15	6	14
None of these	3	2	1
Totals	5057	1664	656

DATA FOR 1993/1994. ADAPTED FROM BROWN, MCCRONE, PATERSON (1996).

RACE AND NATIONAL IDENTITY IN BRITAIN

So far we have examined differences at the level of the constituent nations of the United Kingdom, but there are other conflicts in the British identity. One of the most challenging is race, and its critique of our emphasis on Britishness in the nation is encompassed in the title of one of the most well-known sociological texts on West Indian Culture, *There ain't no black in the Union Jack* (Gilroy 1987).

By the end of the 1950s the number of people in Britain from the Caribbean and South Asia was around 200,000, which was about 0.5 per cent of the British population. The figures from the 1991 Census are shown in Table 13.

Table 13: *Population in Britain by age (in thousands), 1991*								
	UNDER 16	16–24	25–34	35–44	45–54	55–64	65+	ALL AGES
Black Caribbean	109	74	112	51	63	61	28	500
Black African	62	35	60	29	16	7	3	212
Other Black	90	34	33	10	6	3	2	178
Indian	248	128	154	137	84	56	34	840
Pakistani	203	83	68	55	34	25	8	477
Bangladeshi	77	29	19	14	13	9	2	163
Chinese	37	28	36	28	14	9	5	157
Other Asian	48	29	43	43	21	9	5	198
Other ethnic minorities	121	44	52	33	18	12	9	290
White	10027	6509	7783	7264	6104	5473	8714	51874

SOURCE: 1991 CENSUS, OFFICE OF NATIONAL STATISTICS: SOCIAL FOCUS ON ETHNIC MINORITIES (1996) LONDON: HMSO

In 1995 it was estimated by the Labour Force Survey that around 3.2 million people in Britain (5.7 per cent of the total population) were from ethnic minorities. The initial migration came under the terms of the 1948 Nationality Act, when citizens of Britain's colonies and ex-colonies were granted British citizenship and were then free to travel to work and reside in Britain permanently if they so wished (Cashmore 1989). Yet as more migrants followed, the terms of their entry were to be progressively tightened up by the governments which followed. Prime Minster Edward Heath's administration passed the Commonwealth Immigration Act (1971) which restricted migration to heads of households. This did much to restrict families coming in to Britain and slowed the level of immigration from these countries. The development of what has been called by the social commentator, Martin Barker 'the new racism' came from the Conservative government of Margaret Thatcher and was identified with her colleague William Whitelaw. It fixed on genuine fears of losing a 'British way of life'; it had nothing to do with disliking foreigners, but still it created boundaries between 'us' and 'them' (Cashmore 1989).

Points of Evaluation
1 The importance of race to a sense of community should not be underestimated. Too often it is ignored by the modernist theories of nationalism which stress a somewhat Whiggish extension of citizenship rights as their definition of 'successful' nationalism. The rural idyll in England is after all the dream of a white Anglo-Saxon society in Britain.
2 Paul Gilroy has argued that Benedict Anderson's theory is therefore exclusive of race.
3 Rather, says Gilroy (1987), it is the language of war and racism which most forcibly focuses our attention on national boundaries and the entry and exit of black people as they were controlled by the legislation of the time.

Activity
What does the following source tell us about Britain's progress as a multicultural or a multiracial society? Place it in context of the British army's use of a soldier of Afro-Caribbean descent in place of Lord Kitchener in a 1997 version of its most famous call to arms.

... Then [Baroness Thatcher] spotted a model plane featuring BA's new multi-coloured tail logo. The company scrapped the Union flag in favour of a number of ethnic designs – none of which met with the Baroness's approval ... 'We fly the British flag, not these awful things you are putting on tails,' she said ... As she went on describing the designs as 'absolutely terrible', it became clear that BA were content to leave things as they are, so she reached into her famous handbag, pulled out a tissue and wrapped it around the tail of one of the models featuring a design known as Kalahari ... All the while Dennis stood open-mouthed in astonishment at the sheer non-Britishness of the designs. He was heard to mutter: 'For Christ's sake why can't we have British designs.' He was told that some of them were, but it was clear he was still astonished.   (*The Scotsman*, 10 October 1997)

RACE AND NATIONAL IDENTITY IN BRITAIN TODAY

At the Conservative Party Conference held in Brighton in October 1997, the former chairman of the Party Lord Tebbit spoke at a fringe meeting and opened up a debate he had aired in the 1980s. His theme was the pitfall of a multicultural Britain. When first debated, his words were remembered as the 'cricket test'. In this test, he asked those who were themselves of the generations who had left, say, Pakistan, India and the West Indies, where their loyalties lay when these nations played England at international cricket. Did they support England, as the ownership of a British passport would suggest they should, or did they support Pakistan, India or the West Indies, that is, the place of their ethnic origin? Tebbit returned to this theme in 1997 with the following speech:

Multi-culturalism is a divisive force. One cannot uphold two sets of ethnics or be loyal to two nations, any more than a man can have two masters. It perpetuates ethnic divisions because nationality is in the long term more about culture than ethnics. Youngsters of all races should be taught that British history is their history, or they will be forever foreigners holding British passports and the kingdom will become a Yugoslavia.

(*The Guardian*, 8 October 1997)

Compare this argument with recent sociological research on perceptions of Britishness in a Pakistani community in London by Jessica Jacobson (1997). The respondents were all young people of Pakistani descent who were born in Britain or had lived in Britain since they were young children and all possessed British passports.

As the following source shows, Jacobson discovered an extraordinarily wide range of views on what it means to be British and how indeed that judgement is to be made. From this, she argues, there are several widely accepted ways of being 'British'.

'I think I'd have to describe myself first and foremost as a Muslim. I couldn't say I'm British at all.'

'No, not at all [British] ... No! I hope not, anyway. 'Cause I'm not, am I?'

'Yeah, I'm British because I've lived in an English country ... But deep down I'm actually Pakistani.'

'Yes, I do consider myself British. But I don't think that English people would see me as British.'

'Er – yeah, sometimes [I consider myself British]. Depends on the situation.'

'I'm British, I'm obviously born and bred here. But I do consider myself Pakistani – so I'd say I was a British Asian.'

'Predominantly I'm British; I was born here and I've lived here – this is my country.'

'When it comes to cricket, people say – you're from England you should support your English team, no one should support Pakistan, but at the end of the day you've got to support your home country! This [England] *is* our home country ... this is where I was born, but I still end up supporting Pakistan.'

(Jacobson, 1997)

Activity

Jacobson proposes three boundaries which encapsulate race in Britain. Think about these boundaries and then discuss them in class:

• The 'civic boundary' of Britishness. 'This is the formal or official boundary which defines people as British if they are British citizens'.
• The 'racial boundary' of Britishness. This 'defines people as British if they have, or are believed to have, British ancestry or British "blood" '.
• The 'cultural boundary' of Britishness. This 'defines Britishness in terms of values, attitudes and lifestyles: that is, Britishness is regarded as a matter of the culture to which one adheres'.

Study Point

Define a 'cultural boundary'.

SUMMARY

The question 'what does it mean to be British' is clearly a difficult one to answer. The growth in the number of ethnic minorities has confused the situation further. There is no agreed definition of the United Kingdom; many of those living in the 'Celtic fringe' do not feel themselves to be British. The word England is often used to describe the territory which is also inhabited by Welsh, Scots, and Irish. There has been found to be a close relationship between this dual English/British identity among people in England. The history of those others who inhabit connected territories is one, largely, of colonial oppression by the English. Each has expressed their national identity in different ways: Northern Ireland has experienced much political nationalism; in Wales, it has been more cultural; in Scotland, national identity has been tied to the institutions of its civil society. In very recent years attempts are being made to introduce devolution to enable the nations of the United Kingdom to have their own parliament or assemblies: although the nationalist movements have never had full power to determine their nation's future, the change of government in 1997 made this possible. Indeed, MPs in England have raised the issue of regionalism in response to these developments. The growth of ethnic minorities has raised issues of allegiance among some politicians and debate about the concept of multiculturalism. One useful and fruitful attempt to establish what it means to be British has suggested an analysis of civic, racial and cultural boundaries.

STUDY GUIDE

Group work

Debate the inevitability (or not) of the break up of Britain. Divide the class into four, each to take one of the constituent nations of the United Kingdom as its example. Each is to note where a common sense of Britishness prevails and contrast this with a list of where national identity undermines a sense of Britishness. If you would like to get the constitutional positions of the main political parties, write to their head office or local constituency office or log on to their home pages on the World Wide Web:

- **Plaid Cymru**: http://www.wales.com/political-party/plaid-cymru/englishindex.html
- **SNP**: http://www.snp.org.uk/
- **Conservative Party**: http://www.conservative-party.org.uk/
- **Labour Party**: http://www.poptel.org.uk/labour-party/
- **Liberal Democrat Party**: http://www.libdems.org.uk./
- For one view on politics in Northern Ireland, see: **British-Ulster heritage site**: http://www.gpl.net/users/bradley/buhs.html

Coursework

One of the consequences of the 1997 referendum votes in favour of devolution in Scotland and in Wales has been the so-called 'English backlash'. This has taken a number of forms, including a demand that the number of Scottish and Welsh MPs at Westminster be reduced and for the renegotiation of the 'Barnett Formula' which established the proportionate level of block grants to England, Scotland and Wales (but not Northern Ireland).

An example of this backlash was *A Declaration for the North* signed in November 1997 by 52 organisations and 238 individuals. It demanded a directly elected Assembly representing the people of the North of England. The declaration argued that 'Our ability to develop our political, economic and cultural agenda has historically been restrained by the absence of meaningful local power.' (*New Statesman*, 14 November 1997)

There are a number of coursework projects which could be focused around this theme:

- The rise of regional identity in England.
- The prospects for federalism in the United Kingdom (and within Europe).
- The likelihood of an English parliament or a 'northern' parliament.

Nationalism in any of the four nations, or together as 'Britishness', or complicated by race; these are the themes discussed in this chapter. A possible question could ask:

How is contemporary national identity in each of the four nations of the United Kingdom best explained?

The answer would include the following themes: the coherence and the conflict in 'British' identity; the conflation of English and British identity; the historical conflict between Protestant and Catholic over land in Northern Ireland; the cultural basis of Welsh national identity; the importance of church, law and education to Scottish civil society; race and national identity.

From this chapter, you should now understand the following themes. Take time to make a key concept card on each:

- The United Kingdom of Great Britain and Northern Ireland: why Yookay and Ukania? The relative threats to the survival of the British 'nation-state'.
- The 'absence' of nationalism in England/Britain.
- The key national histories of England, Northern Ireland, Wales and Scotland.
- Race and nationality identity in Britain since the Second World War, its differences and its similarities – 'the cricket test'.

1 Discuss the problems which sociologists identify in using a term such as 'British nation-state'. Consider the issues in relation to the need for national identity.
2 Critically assess the cultural and social similarities and differences between Welsh, Scottish and Irish Nationalists.

8

UNEVEN DEVELOPMENT

Introduction

THIS CHAPTER CONTINUES to emphasise the stresses and the strains of 'British' national identity, concentrating on both the internal and the external challenges to the British 'nation-state'. In the previous chapter we introduced the key variables behind the creation and maintenance of unique national identities in each of the nations of the United Kingdom. We outlined the differences between nations, and between the different races in the United Kingdom, and explained how these make it difficult to think in terms of a coherent British nation-state – there is one British state which encompasses a range of national identities. Still, 'Britishness' permeates into these national identities. The grief apparent throughout Britain at the death of Diana, Princess of Wales in 1997 is a case in point. Elton John's reworking of his song *Candle in the Wind*, released to raise funds for charities associated with the Princess, has despite its Anglo-centric sentiment sold over 4.5 million copies in Britain alone and has broken all previous records for the biggest selling single.

There is also a sense in which the ethnic and cultural differences of the constituent nations, particularly the 'Celtic' nations, are becoming less distinctive than they once were. With each passing year the nations of Scotland, Wales and Northern Ireland are becoming more like their large neighbour England. This is referred to as the process of 'Anglicisation'. An important consequence of this process is that England has achieved a measure of 'internal colonialism'. We will examine the reactions of the peripheral nations to England's internal colonialism through Anglicisation.

It is not just within Britain that cultural differences are disappearing. This chapter will conclude with a discussion of whether or not cultural differences throughout the world are being eroded. The term 'McDonaldisation' has been coined by George Ritzer to explain this process.

Table 14: *Theorists, concepts and issues in this chapter*		
KEY THEORISTS	KEY CONCEPTS	KEY ISSUES
Wallerstein	Core	Why do core nations develop?
	Periphery	Why do peripheral nations lag behind?
	Cultural division of labour	Why does Gellner argue that nationalism is a response to economic inequalities?
Gunder Frank	Neo-colonialism	Why are former colonies still economically tied to core nations? Are the terms of this trade unfair?
Webster	Critique of Frank	Are Third World nations really exploited?
Hechter	Diffusion model	All culture looks increasingly like that of the core nation – 'acculturation'.
	Internal colonial model	The periphery rediscovers its identity to resist economic and social acculturation; but is it exploited by the core?
	The Celtic Fringe	Is there a common 'Celtic experience'?
Nairn	Relative over-development	Did Scotland do well out of the Union of 1707 and did the discovery of oil off Scottish shores create a new form of nationalism?
Ritzer	McDonaldisation	Is this a new cultural form?
Jarvie and Walker	90-minute patriots	Does sport neuter political nationalism?

CORE AND PERIPHERY

The key issue which connects our discussion of the break up of Britain in the previous chapter, and the many fundamental challenges to the nation-state which will be discussed here and in our final chapter, is that of core and periphery. For the United Kingdom these concepts can be explained as:

- Core – England
- Periphery – Scotland, Wales, Northern Ireland

In *The Modern World Systems* (1989, NY Academic Press) Immanuel Wallerstein provides one of the most powerful analyses of core and periphery in the world today. He argues that inequalities between core nations and peripheral nations result in a 'cultural division of labour'. Skill and employment differences, segregated by religion in the Belfast shipyards, is one good example of what this means. Another is the way in which multinational companies send their assembly and component work to low-wage economies around the globe, keeping the high status and well-paid management and research employment within their core nation, to which all profits flow. This creates employment in disadvantaged areas, but it is the type of work which will never allow, for instance, the Third World to catch up economically with the First World.

Central to Wallerstein's analysis is 'why do core nations develop?'. Why, for instance, was Britain the first industrial nation? What was different in Britain from the social and economic conditions in France or Germany which caused them to lag behind? The subtlety in Wallerstein's argument is that he insists there are not multiple capitalist states but only one capitalist world system. Nation-states developed as a response to this economic system. England/Britain was ideally placed from the sixteenth century onwards to exploit this world-system to the maximum advantage (see Greenfeld and Kohn in Chapters 6 and 7).

As we saw in the work of Ernest Gellner in Chapter 5 the role of nation-states in the capitalist world system was to result in inequalities between nations. Some, especially those with favoured trading relationships with their colonies, did better than others and this contributed to nationalism. It was what Gellner called the 'uneven geography of development' which contributed to nationalism throughout the world as nations resorted to nationalism as a political means of overcoming unequal economic relationships.

In many of the works analysing the Third World and the less developed nations, this relationship of inequality is attributed to unequal terms of trade with the developed countries. The term is 'neo-colonialism'. Because these poorer countries are no longer colonies, and are generally republics, the old relationships of exploitation have gone only to be replaced, it is argued by proponents of this view, by new forms. Webster (1984) quotes Nkrumah, President of Ghana in the 1960s, for the definition of neo-colonialism: 'The essence of neo-colonialism is that the state which is subject to it is, in theory, independent and has all the trappings of international sovereignty. In reality its economic system and thus its internal policy is directed from the outside'.

Andre Gunder Frank developed the theory of neo-colonialism or 'under-development' to its logical extreme. He argued that it led to a specialisation of production in the Third World by concentrating on a limited range of primary exports. These were goods which were subject to the volatility of international markets and which tended to offer low wages and were labour intensive.

Points of Evaluation

1 Webster outlines a critique of Gunder Frank's model. He points out that it is somewhat vague and assumes that the Third World is static in its relationships with the developed world.

2 It is argued by critics of Frank that the focus should not be on how the surplus is extracted, but on how it can be developed for greater profits.

3 Like Gellner's uneven geography of development theory of nationalism, followed also by theorists such as Hroch and Nairn, underdevelopment theory is too inflexible to cope with particular empirical realities, yet the premise of the argument remains influential.

Activity
In what ways, if at all, can it be argued that the developed world 'exploits' the developing world? Can the terms of trade between such countries ever be turned in favour of the primary producing nation?

ACCULTURATION

One of the key issues of the core and periphery relationship is the argument that not only is the peripheral area likely to find its economy immature in comparison with the core, but that the cultural values of the core begin to take over and dominate – a process known as acculturation. This issue can be seen most clearly if we consider Britain as our example before taking on board the implications at an international level.

To many it seemed strange that Scotland should vote decisively for its own parliament with tax-raising powers in 1997, a decade short of three centuries after voluntarily dismantling its parliament, as England did, in order to create the parliament of Great Britain. Surely 300 years is enough time for the Scots and the English to compromise on a stable British identity? Especially so, it would seem, because this Union took place before the age of nationalism, as defined by the modernists, and because the British monarchy and the British state was not reticent in making use of symbols, ceremonies and occasions which, as we have seen, are encapsulated in Hobsbawm's term 'invented tradition'.

Looking in particular at the social and economic development of Britain from the sixteenth century to the twentieth century, Michael Hechter's book *Internal Colonialism* (1975, Routledge) is similar to the ideas of the underdevelopment theorists. In this book Hechter makes two very interesting points:

- That there are two models of national developments: the 'diffusion' model, and the 'internal colonial' model.
- That Scotland, Wales and Ireland comprise a common 'Celtic fringe' to England's core.

THE DIFFUSION MODEL OF NATIONAL DEVELOPMENT

In the *diffusion* model it is argued that there will, throughout the industrial period, be an increasing interaction between the core and the periphery leading to eventual equalisation.

Hechter argues that in this model acculturation occurs – the development of common culture – and it is perceived to happen automatically when two groups have first hand knowledge of each other. Contemporary examples of this include the endings of the Cold War – when 'suddenly' there was greater understanding between the United States of America and the USSR, and the ending of religious segregation in employment and schooling in Northern Ireland, breaking the isolation of opposing groups.

Activity

The start of this process of developing a common culture can be ascertained from the sources which follow. Write 100 words on why the English language has been so important to maintaining cultural coherence in Britain.

THE CULTURAL PRE-EMINENCE OF THE ENGLISH LANGUAGE

The fusion of all the inhabitants of these islands into one homogeneous, English-speaking whole, the breaking down of barriers between us, the swallowing up of several provincial nationalities, is a consummation to which the natural course of things irresistibly tends; it is a necessity of what is called civilisation.

(Matthew Arnold 1867)

GWYNFOR WILLIAMS, THE FORMER LEADER OF PLAID CYMRU, 1981

What is Britishness? The first thing to realise is that it is another word for Englishness; it is a political word which arose from the existence of the British state and which extends Englishness over the lives of the Welsh, the Scots and the Irish. If one asks what the difference is between English culture and British culture one realises that there is no difference. They are the same. The British language is the English language. British education is English education. British television is English television. The British press is the English press. The British Crown is the English Crown, and the Queen of Britain is the Queen of England. The British Constitution is called by Dicey, the main authority of the subject, 'the English Constitution'. The British Parliament is that which is termed in Kenneth Mackenzie's authoritative book, *The English Parliament*. The English language is the only language it is permitted to speak here. There is no British law – there is only English and Scottish Law. Britishness is Englishness.

(Quoted in Bassnett 1997)

Study Point
Why is the maintenance of the Welsh language seen as so important that some nationalists have painted out English names on signposts?

Points of Evaluation

1 Arguably the whole world is trying to be like the First World. Wherever you go in the world you can get a McDonald's meal and a can of Coca Cola. Once consumed they create the same litter in Nairobi and Budapest as on Sunset Boulevard. Cultural influences like popular music or Hollywood are also immense: from Disney to Schwarzenegger, Stallone and Spielberg, American films are sub-titled or more usually dubbed in cinemas everywhere. There is then a sense of increasing homogeneous global culture, one that is American-led.

2 There is much to be said for this model; culturally we are all becoming more alike. Language is, of course, the main vehicle of this diffusion, especially English across a range of nations (although Chinese remains the language most commonly spoken in the world).

3 The power of English, spoken and written 'correctly' was an important part of education both within Britain and in its colonies, especially India and Africa.

THE INTERNAL COLONIAL MODEL

But to return to Michael Hechter and the second model he proposes: the *internal colonial* model.

In this thesis the core dominates the periphery politically and through this relationship it is then able to exploit it materially. This situation arises, it is argued, because of the uneven wave of modernisation in state territories. Hechter argues that when peripheral industrialisation does occur, if at all, it tends to be highly specialised – filling a need for the core area – or it tends to be more export–orientated – the twentieth century development of multinational companies and their exploitation of branch plants in peripheral areas is a good example of this.

While the diffusion model predicts a lessening of regional economic difficulties, the internal colonial model predicts that these will persist or increase. As you might expect from the title he chose for this book, Hechter believed that the internal colonial model was the more relevant one.

• He argued that the process of assimilation was always slower than the diffusion model had predicted. Britain has been part of the European Union for over 20 years; but few regard themselves as European not British.

- Traditional culture in the periphery was more enduring than expected – it resisted assimilation into the wider culture of the core area. Gaelic and Welsh language revival movements, especially in the 1880s and throughout the twentieth century, are testament to this.
- In the research he did on the industrial economies of peripheral areas – particularly of the peripheral nations in the United Kingdom – Hechter argues that they exhibited the characteristics of the internal colonial model: their industrial production tended to be complementary to the needs of the metropolis.

Points of Evaluation

1 'Internal colonialism' is analogous to the relationship between the First World and the Third World, which we saw in the 'underdevelopment school' of Andre Gunder Frank.
2 It sustains the argument that the peripheral (or the colonial) country often specialises in the production of a narrow range of primary commodities and raw materials for export to the First World – or more usually the mother country.
3 That analogy is fair, but we must remember to be careful in our discussion of the core.
4 As Neil Evans (1989) has pointed out for the United Kingdom, the core is the south east of England, not 'England'.
5 He notes that it is also possible to refer to an *economic* core and a *political* core. The combined weight of Manchester, Leeds, Bradford, Sheffield and Hull seemed to tip the balance of the economic core to the north of England during the Industrial Revolution and for a long time beyond. Cardiff, Belfast and Glasgow also were economic leaders in the latter phase of the Industrial Revolution.
6 As we saw in the last chapter, England is not a unified nation. Peter Taylor's phrase (1991) the 'Crown heartland' of the south east – Mrs Thatcher's Little England – is symbolic of the wider social and cultural dominance of England.

Activity
Where is the core in the United Kingdom? Indeed, is there only one? A very good starting place is John Osmond (1988) *The Divided Kingdom* (London: Constable) which develops a discussion of regionalism within Britain and contains many useful maps and figures.

Internal colonialism and nationalism

Hechter quotes approvingly Gellner's argument that 'the initial advantage to one cultural group or another was an historical accident caused by the uneven spread of development'. Hence the link to nationalism – economic superiority led to cultural superiority in territorial areas which became core nations.

Not only is nationalism a response to uneven prosperity between nations, but it is a response to what, the model predicts, will become increasing deprivation. Thus, Hechter suggests, the periphery will typically have:

* a declining population (young migrate to core; fertility decline);
* an ageing population (similarly, due to migration of the young);
* a predominantly female population (as it is the males who are the more likely to migrate temporarily for seasonal work, or on a permanent basis, reflecting the lack of employment opportunities).

This is a self-perpetuating disadvantage – a disadvantage that is cumulative. The population cannot reproduce itself, it cannot sustain itself, there are too many dependants and too few producers.

Activity
This argument concentrates on unequal relationships between nations, but equally it can be powerfully used to analyse regional differences within nations. Go back to the analysis carried out on the rural communities discussed in Chapters 2 and 3 and complete a checklist on whether these communities are regionally disadvantaged within their nation.

THE CELTIC FRINGE

Hechter's idea of the Celtic fringe is as intuitively understandable as it is difficult to sustain. The idea is that the Scots and the Welsh and, more problematically, the Irish also, can be grouped under the common title of a Celtic fringe – and that they all had a similar experience of being dominated by an English core.

An important component in Hechter's notion of the Celtic fringe is what he identifies as two distinct Celtic languages in Britain (which are not mutually understandable):

* q-Celtic (Irish, Manx and Scottish Gaelic)
* p-Celtic (Welsh, Cornish, and in France, Breton)

This is interesting, yet we would argue that the divisions within these two constructs are equally as great, and this linguistic divide is not a useful way of thinking about Great Britain. There is, then, a danger in this concept. But where Hechter is much stronger is in his argument that the Celtic fringe has evolved historically along ecological lines – based on the distribution of high and low land in the British Isles. The lowlands tended (as they are today) to have an arable/mixed economy whereas the highland territories were mainly pastoral – and therefore poorer.

Hechter points out that this ecological balance existed prior to the expansion of the English state in the sixteenth century. The implication of this is that England became a core nation to the Celtic periphery, and maintained its position as such (thus practising internal colonialism), because it was able to maintain and enforce this ecological balance. Indeed the unions with Wales in 1536 and with Scotland in 1707 were all about administering trade and the supply of food. For example, one of the many reasons why the Scots opted for the Union of 1707 was because of the threat that they would be increasingly excluded from the English home market and the markets of the Empire; by Union, the Scots secured the biggest free trade zone in Europe at the time. Meanwhile Union with Ireland in 1801 was the continuation of two centuries of subjugation of Catholicism by the Anglican and Presbyterian settlers.

Activity
Is the idea of the Celtic fringe still valid today? Think of levels in internal migration and migration from overseas; think also of the level of intermarriage within Britain between couples born in, for example, England and Scotland. You might like to get some migration figures from the Office of National Statistics whose publications can be found in some larger libraries, by writing to their information office or through the WWW at http://www.emap.co.uk/ons.

Internal colonialism reversed? Relative over-development

So far we have argued that Tom Nairn is in the same camp as Wallerstein, Gellner and Hechter in that he lays great emphasis on the uneven geography of development being the raw material which the French Revolution then built upon to create nationalism as a political movement, and so to respond to dependency.

But Nairn adds an important layer upon his explanation of Scotland's national identity since the eighteenth century. Uneven development should have led to Scottish nationalism; that it did not follow the political mobilisation of Europe in the 1780s and 1790s or in 1848 and the early 1850s was, he argues, because of Scotland's favourable socio-economic position. The point for Nairn is that the strong external state control allowed Scottish civil society the breathing space to develop free from the normal pressures of uneven capitalist development. Scotland experienced industrialisation quickly and early, in conjunction with the first industrial nation. This was unusual for most small nations and was to Scotland's economic benefit (McCrone 1992).

Scotland's sense of national identity is strong, yet the language is less widely spoken than Welsh is in Wales. Suggest some ways in which this sense of national identity is maintained in Scotland.

Scotland was not simply the 'periphery' to England's economic 'core'. It was because Scottish civil society had advanced so far and so quickly, and because the new bourgeois social classes inherited a socio-economic position at a unique historical juncture vastly more favourable to that of any backward nationality, that there was no need for parliamentary nationalism. If it had not been for this particular set of circumstances the uneven spread of capitalism, which contributed to political nationalism elsewhere in Europe, would probably have occurred in Scotland. Nairn (1981) terms the result in Scotland 'cultural sub-nationalism' – a sort of deformed nationalism; the result was an inferior culture and identity – a cultural neurosis. Certain sectors in the Scottish economy were doing so well out of the Union that political nationalism was 'bought off'. The resulting cultural identity has been termed as sub-nationalism because of its inability to underpin nation-statehood for Scotland (Morton 1998b).

This argument came full-circle in the 1970s with the discovery of North Sea oil. This fuelled a new Scottish nationalism based on the belief that Scotland would be economically better off if it were independent (ie if the profits and taxes from oil production went to a Scottish exchequer not a Westminster one). The argument has become full-circle because Nairn calls this 'relative over-development'! In a sense, nationalists felt Scotland had now become the economic core (although this was never reality, as England is so much bigger).

McDONALDISATION

No matter the unevenness in development, there is a growing awareness that we are all part of a global culture. We have talked of England being the core nation to the Celtic periphery, yet all are peripheral to the cultural (and of course economic) dominance of the United States and Japan (a theme we pick up in more detail in our final chapter). The phrase 'McDonaldisation' was coined by George Ritzer as a means of analysing how 'the process by which the principles of the fast-food restaurant are coming to dominate more and more sectors of American society as well as of the rest of the world'. The phrase is also indicative of acculturation, in this case American-led.

McDonald's has achieved its exalted position because virtually all Americans, and many others, have passed through its golden arches on innumerable occasions. Furthermore, most of us have been bombarded with commercials extolling McDonald's virtues, commercials that are tailored to different audiences. Some play to young children watching Saturday-morning cartoons. Others solicit young adults watching prime-time programs. Still others coax grandparents to take their grandchildren to McDonald's ... A poll of school-age children showed that 96% of them could identify Ronald McDonald, second only to Santa Claus in name recognition.

(Ritzer 1996)

Activity
List all the features of American and Japanese culture which are now everyday features of life in Britain. Think also in terms of the goods that we buy, as well as the films that we watch. To what extent is 'British' culture being undermined by these two influential nations? You might like to find the official McDonald's home page on the WWW and then compare it with the hundreds if not thousands of unofficial, and often hostile, McDonald's web sites. How indicative are these sites of American acculturation?

SUMMARY

There is a debate as to whether there is a process of acculturation developing within the area we refer to as the United Kingdom. Are the Scots, Northern Irish and the Welsh at the periphery, becoming more like their larger neighbour at the core? The dominant culture, promoted through the mass media, is that of England. This process has been termed internal colonialism, Anglicisation. It is typified in the more global effects of McDonaldisation. Sociologists have debated these issues and two main models have emerged, those of 'diffusion' (which predicts increasing commonality) and 'internal colonial' (which predicts that the core will increasingly predominate). Sometimes, as in the case of Scotland, peripheral nations can do relatively well in their relationships with a core nation, but not uniformly so. The core nation itself can also be stratified between an economic core and a political core. Where more agreement is possible is over the increasing power of the global market to influence cultural attitudes. McDonald's, in particular, as well as many other international shops and fast-food chains, has had a powerful effect on producing cultural uniformity.

STUDY GUIDE

Group work

The theme of uneven development in Britain and in the wider world forms the group work for this chapter. Divide the class into two. Group A should concentrate on the economic development of the constituent nations of the United Kingdom; Group B should look at the economic development of one or two selected countries of the Third World and compare them with the overall British and American figures. GDP or average earnings/cost of living figures could be looked at. In the first instance, each group should identify the main contrasts from what they have read in this chapter. This will provide a theoretical explanation for why differences should be expected. To gain further information on these contrasts, consult any of the many statistical sources available. *Regional Trends* for the United Kingdom would be a good starting place for Group A, as would the *Labour Force Survey*. For Group B, the Office of National Statistics could be looked at, and the statistical services of the European Community and United Nations.

Coursework

Football, as a world sport, is claimed to channel and handle nationalism, to neutralise it. The so-called '90-minute patriots' thesis is our focus. It suggests that sport provides a harmless outlet for nationalist feeling, especially in Britain, and this avoids the build-up of more 'harmful' political discontent.

The role of sport in national identity can be systematised in what the sociologists Jarvie and Walker (1994) describe as the most common arguments:

- 'That sport is inherently conservative and that it helps to consolidate official or centre nationalism, patriotism and racism'.
- 'That sport has some inherent property that makes it an instrument of national unity and integration, for example, in peripheral or emerging nations'.
- 'That sport helps to reinforce national consciousness and cultural nationalism'.
- 'That sport provides a safety-valve or outlet of emotional energy for frustrated peoples or nations'.
- 'That sport has at times contributed to unique political struggle some of which have been closely connected to nationalist politics and nationalist struggles'.
- 'That sport, whether it be through nostalgia, mythology, invented or selected traditions, contributes to a quest for identity be it local, regional, cultural or global'.

How valid is the thesis that most of us are 90-minute patriots in Britain today, and which of the arguments identified by Jarvie and Walker is most relevant to your nation?

The nature of core and periphery relationships, acculturation, underdevelopment in the Third World, relative over-development, and sport and nationalism are all themes on which questions could be based. An example might be:

How useful is the concept of core and periphery to understanding nationalism in contemporary societies?

Some of the themes you should include in an answer are definitions and examples of core nations and peripheral nations; an acceptance of multiple and split cores; the relationship between the First and the Third World; the concept of relative over-development; an understanding of the main features of nationalism in one or two case studies. Chapter 7 provides you with much case-study material for Britain.

From this chapter, you should now understand the following themes. Take time to make a key concept card on each:

- Core and periphery.
- World systems theory (Wallerstein).
- Internal colonialism in Britain (Hechter).
- The Celtic Fringe.
- Relative over- and under-development.
- Conflict between the First World and the Third World; the specialisation of production.
- Acculturation: English, American (Japanese).
- Sport and national identity.

1 'Nationalism is a response to economic inequalities'. Discuss and evaluate this view.
2 Evaluate different models and theories which have been used by sociologists to explain differences between 'developed' and 'underdeveloped' societies.

9

GLOBALISATION: MULTIPLE LOCALITIES, MULTIPLE IDENTITIES

Introduction

THIS CONCLUDING CHAPTER will stress the coexistence of multiple localities and multiple identities within Britain. The continued relevance of national identity in each of the four nations, as well as the variety of challenges to 'Britishness' within the global era, demonstrates that the end of community and of locality is not inevitable. Increasingly the home community sits uncomfortably alongside pan-European and other more global identities. This unease has been facilitated by dramatic changes in the 'networked society', centralising and decentralising our localities simultaneously.

The global village is now a reality, but its consequence has been that ethnic diversity is reinvigorated with new powers. The localities in which we live are far from uniform. Different national identities have increased in significance rather than declined (as one might expect) through globalisation. The nation-state may be under threat, but arguably nationalism is the word which defines the twentieth century. Alongside that concept, however, is another: identity. Within civil society, where localities and communities abound, new forms of identity are being made and re-made.

Table 15: *Theorists, concepts and issues in this chapter*		
KEY THEORISTS	KEY CONCEPTS	KEY ISSUES
McGrew Harvey	Globalisation 'Time–space compression'	What are the consequences of becoming part of a global economy and global political order?
Hall	National differences eroded. Rise of local identities. Hybrid national identities.	Is the nation-state dead?
Held	State sovereignty undermined	Is global acculturation the result?
Morton	Fragmented national identities	How are national histories now made 'authentic', if at all?
Smith	Pan-European identity	Why such resistance to a European identity?
Mann	Society and economy have always been linked	Is globalisation over-stated?
Sudjic	Locality	What are the similarities between an airport and a city?
	Community	The golden age and the rural idyll still persist in our desire to seek out a 'community'. Why?
	Nation	*Gemeinschaft* and *Gesellschaft* still retain much significance in structuring how we think of ourselves and of others.
Moss	Networked society	Are new forms of community being created through the World Wide Web?

GLOBALISATION

In this final chapter we introduce two themes which have in recent years changed fundamentally how we relate to our own personal locality and community.

- The end of the 'nation state?'
- The fragmentation of (national) identity?

These ideas are discussed within the concept of 'globalisation', one of the most powerful sets of analyses of recent developments within modernity and of the transition to post-modernity. Both are presented as questions, because they remain highly contentious issues. Their discussion will lead us to explore what future remains for the locality and the community. First of all, we need to understand what is meant by the concept of globalisation. A useful definition is provided by McGrew:

Globalisation refers to the multiplicity of linkages and interconnections that transcend the nation-states (and by implication the societies) which make up the modern world system. It defines a process through which events, decisions, and activities in one part of the world can come to have quite significant consequences for individuals and communities in quite distant parts of the globe. Nowadays, goods, capital, people, knowledge, images, communications, crime, culture, pollutants, drugs, fashions, and beliefs all readily flow across territorial boundaries.

(McGrew 1992)

Points of Evaluation

1 But as McGrew tells us, globalisation is much more than just increased interconnectedness. It is about breaking geography, creating, in the terminology of Anthony Giddens, 'absence' from our everyday localities.

2 With the link broken between time and place, our everyday lives are no longer shaped by when the post office is open, or when half day closing or the local public holiday is upon us.

3 Increasingly we are governed by other time zones, other international events. The internet, electronic mail, the telephone, voice mail, the cellular phone, the fax machine: these are the means by which we communicate.

4 The British economy is heavily interconnected with the stock markets of the United States and the Far East while it is possible to interact with sporting events as they happen all over the world.

5 This introduces us to the idea of the 'global village' which seems to be defined by this level of interconnectedness. In each case the external time pressure on our localities produces, in the words of the social theorist Charles Harvey, 'bursts of intense time-space compression'.

THE CONSEQUENCES OF GLOBALISATION

There is a 'stretching' and 'deepening' of our communities because of the changes that we have termed 'globalisation'. But how different is this phenomenon? As the saying goes, no man is an island! We must not forget the interconnectedness of the capitalist world system from the sixteenth century onwards, the theme of Immanuel Wallerstein's analysis (Chapter 8). As Stuart Hall (1992) reminds us, globalisation is not new. But, he adds, there is no doubt that globalisation is inherent in modernity. Economically it has been Japan and the United States than have led the way, as Fujita explains.

As the globalisation of the Japanese economy proceeds, Tokyo has become an increasingly important centre for international trade, innovation and finance. Japanese companies account for nearly half of the total value of the global top 1000 companies (Business Week, 1989). Some 345 Japanese companies account for 47% of the total value of these companies while 353 American companies account for 32.4%. (1991: 277).

(Fujita 1991)

Activity
Examine the town or area in which you live or study and note the possible evidence for the impact of globalisation on the economy.

Globalisation is about international economics, of companies whose value is greater than the GNP of many medium-sized nations. Globalisation is also about a new level of interaction across the globe, bringing new communities of users to our terminals. We cannot but deal with globalisation as one of the most fundamental challenges to locality and community precisely because, almost by definition, it undermines the nation-state. It cracks open the coherence of time and place in the geographically bounded nation-state. The power of the globalisation process is in its stretching and deepening of time and of our political and social experiences.

Stuart Hall (1992) has identified three possible consequences of globalisation:

• National identities are being eroded as a result of the growth of cultural homogenisation and 'the global postmodern'.
• Cultural and other 'local' or particularistic identities are being strengthened by the resistance to globalisation.
• National identities are declining but new identities of hybridity are taking their place.

GLOBALISATION AND THE 'NATION-STATE'

David Held (1996) has analysed the end of the nation-state in the face of globalisation in terms of the loss of sovereignty. By this he means that the loss of the nation-state's ability to determine its own future has increasingly undermined its coherence.

He identifies four disjunctures where this process is occurring:

• the emergence of a complex international division of labour for global profitability where markets and societies are becoming more sensitive to each other;
• between the state as an autonomous force in military terms and a world of supranational organisations, such as NATO, the United Nations and the European Community;
• the many international organisations which manage international finance, trade, ecological directives and aid.
• the undermining of the idea of the citizen of the nation-state by international law which may go beyond territorial jurisdiction.

Points of Evaluation

1 These points encapsulate neatly the challenge of supranational organisations to the integrity of the nation–state in its law-making as well as its cultural distinctiveness.
2 How often are challenges to British law referred to Europe for an ultimate, more 'politically neutral', decision?
3 How anachronistic is Black Rod in a world of Brussels bureaucrats?
4 How can, for example, a family-owned chain of sports shops survive in a world where brand-name suppliers have the power to dictate the terms on which their products are sold, at what price and by whom?
5 These features point to a loss of legal, political and commercial sovereignty in the nation-state, followed by, as we have seen, global acculturation.

GLOBALISATION AND NATIONAL IDENTITY

The second area of dramatic change under the dynamic of globalisation is in identity. Both the many social identities people possess and the British national identity are increasingly fragmented. Take, for instance, the filming of the Oscar-winning *Braveheart*, the story of the thirteenth-century Scottish freedom fighter, and directed by its Hollywood star: 'Mel Gibson (b. 1956, Peekshill, New York, emigrated to Australia in 1968, five feet and ten inches in height) to play Sir William Wallace (b. 1270?, Elderslie, Scotland, six feet and seven inches in height) in a film financed from institutional investors in America and shot on location primarily in Ireland' (Morton 1996b). What passes for 'authenticity' here is undoubtedly open for debate.

Sir William Wallace, Liberator of Scotland (reproduced with permission of the Smith Art Gallery, Stirling)

To look at the fragmentation of identity in another way, our solidarity with colleagues at work is no longer based around familial or community recruitment (as the shipyards and many regiments of the British army used to be). Our demand for gender and other equalities is a matter for European legislation rather than occasional enlightened employer paternalism. 'Who we are' is no longer the same as when our cultural values were first broadcast by television from Alexandra Palace by the BBC in 1936. Satellite television has brought in cultural experiences from around the globe, particularly of national sporting occasions. Many football fans in England may now identify more with the superstars of the Italian, French and Spanish leagues than with England's cricketers or Rugby Union side. 'Who are we?' is increasingly complex, although as we shall see, it does not necessarily follow that national identity is any less secure: its construction is just different.

Study Point
When Celtic became the first British football club to win the European Cup in 1967, all their players were born in the Glasgow area. Consider what it means today to 'support' a major football team which consists entirely of players from different countries and areas of Britain.

Stuart Hall has argued that for the postmodern individual, identity is no longer fixed, it has become a movable feast (1992). It is something that is very temporary, to do with personal and national history, and 'any one of a range of identities would be used, although only usually for a short period before a new identity becomes fashionable'. Take, for example, the recent troubles experienced by the House of Windsor. Its role as perhaps the most comprehensive and all-encompassing historical tradition, representing many of the core cultural values of England/Britain over generations, has come to be increasingly less relevant. Ironically, the immense and remarkably surprising public grief for the early death of Diana, Princess of Wales, reflects appreciation for a figure then outside the monarchical core. Indeed, press comment that Charles engaged in a 'charm offensive' by 'doing a Diana' at royal functions subsequent to the funeral of his former wife, are testament to the flexibility of traditional culture when faced with a need to modernise. To summarise, in the words of Stuart Hall: 'the nation is a system of cultural presentations and these representations face a new level of re-creation if national identity is to survive'. So far, successful re-creation has not eluded the core institutions of British nationality.

Indeed, a sense of European-ness is hard to find despite the power of the supranational organisations and the prospect of a single European currency. As

Smith has pointed out, there are too few common myths and memories that are not based around war between *these* nations. Thus he argues, nationalism has pre-empted pan-Europeanism as the dominant identity:

Its shrines and monuments are everywhere. They occupy the official centre – in the Arches of Triumph and the tombs of the Unknown Soldier – and the many popular peripheries. The nation's statutary, its flags and emblems, its temples and memorials, dominate the hills, fill the squares and decorate the town halls, reminding the citizens of their allegiance and evoking their pride. Beside these memorials of stone, what has 'Europe' been able to offer? Can its emblems evoke the same passions as those of its nations?

(Smith 1995)

Perhaps it is ironic that Smith should use examples of nationalist sentiment (monuments and tombs) from the empirical lists of the modernist, since his argument for the persistence of national identity in the face of globalisation is premised on the ethnic uniqueness of the constituent nations of Europe. But if we ignore this splitting of hairs, then we can appreciate that Smith's argument is powerful. The modernists may dominate the academic literature, yet it is difficult for the most modern of identities, a pan-European one, to shake off its innumerable historical pasts. As Smith concludes, the nation remains indispensable to our networked society: 'For a global culture seems unable to offer the qualities of collective faith, dignity and hope that only a "religion surrogate", with its promise of territorial culture-community across the generations, can provide'.

So we must be clear, then, that the 'nation-state' is under challenge, but not yet at an end. In the case of Britain, it is apparent that even with the signing of the Maastricht Treaty in 1991, its politicians remain undecided on whether to enter into full social and economic integration with its European partners, particularly with the single currency, or whether Britain could still 'go it alone'. These were the issues which split the Conservative government throughout the 1990s and facilitated its defeat in the 1997 general election.

Points of Evaluation

1 Is the concept of globalisation over-stated? Sklair's survey (1995) of the sociological use of this term has concluded that there has tended to be a dual focus: on transnational corporations and the technical base of the mass media.
2 We have already argued that national identity – in terms of its core cultural institutions – has not been lost, just reinvented when necessary. Perhaps, then, the effects of globalisation are over-stated?
3 Michael Mann argues that the nation-state is not in any general decline despite losing out, to some extent, to supranational organisations. He argues that the nation-state 'is still gaining at the expense of the local, the regional, and especially the private forces'.
4 Mann, like Wallerstein and Hall, points out that 'society' has *never* been merely national. 'Transnational relations are not merely "postmodern": they

have always undercut the sovereignty of all states' (Mann 1996).

5   The example of the many nation-states which were economically dependent
    on the United States and USSR in the years following the end of the Second
    World War is apposite here.

Activity

To explore the arguments identified in this section undertake two short exercises:

1   Will the European Union mean the end for the British nation-state? The British
    Social Attitudes Survey for 1995/6 found a growing acceptance of Britain's
    membership of the European Union but a general cooling in the wish for greater
    integration, especially following the signing of the Maastricht Treaty in 1991. How
    would you explain this view?
2   What does it mean to be a member of an ethnic minority in Britain today? What
    has been the challenge of the globalisation process to identities formed in the
    earlier part of the twentieth century?

For each topic write 50–100 words examining the continued survival of the British
national identity, and the British nation-state's sovereignty, in the age of globalisation.

GLOBALISATION AND LOCALITY, COMMUNITY AND NATION

As well as sustaining a new challenge for the nation-state and the construction of
identity, developments in the modern economy and industry have had profound
effects on our cities, towns and villages, as well as our communities. The
imperatives of capitalist growth, gentrification in our large urban settlements,
allied to the development of what has been termed the 'networked society', can
be seen to have effected a new sense of place. In the introduction to this chapter
we stressed that globalisation broke the bonds between time and place, with
developments in communication taking the lead role. Our task now is to explore
how globalisation has impacted on our physical localities and on our sense of
locality, community and nation today.

LOCALITY: THE AIRPORT AS CITY SQUARE

In Chapter 5 we introduced 'edge city' as the most dramatic development in the
modern city. We extend that theme now by looking at the work of Dejan Sudjic
(1992). Sudjic analyses the ways in which new sets of social relationships arise
from such changes in our urban localities. He takes Heathrow Airport as one of
his examples by perceiving it as a city in its own right. It has a substantial
demand for unskilled labour, employing over 58,000 people in the early 1990s,

plus an estimated 300,000 other jobs which exist because of it. Indeed, it is Heathrow Airport – particularly its sheer size – which makes London an international city, handling more passengers than Paris and Frankfurt combined (its two nearest rivals).

For Sudjic the airport has many characteristics of the city: 'it attracts tourists and plane spotters, job hunters and salesmen, criminals, retailers and caterers. Businessmen come here for conferences. Punjabi women from nearby Southall find work as cleaners and kitchen staff ... The Wapping paparazzi keep the place permanently staked out on watch for passing celebrities. Clearly this is as highly charged a part of the public realm as Trafalgar Square'. All Heathrow lacks, he argues, is residential housing, and only then if you exclude the hotel residents. There are many shops in the major airports of the world, not just the duty free. Airports are fast becoming places just to visit for their facilities, as well as providing a means of transport. According to the British Airports Authority, one in five passengers who use the bus stops at Heathrow will never use a plane.

The international airport is symbolic of a number of our key themes in this book:

- It is a new locality in the twentieth century, a new form of service centre, creating new sets of social relationships.
- It is a new form of 'city' planted in the countryside. Most international airports are on the outskirts of cities. They attract communication routes, service providers, hotels and housing. If the urban and the rural world are at two poles on a continuum, the airport is blurring their boundaries.
- It has become a community in its own right through the people that work there, continually fly from there, stop there, commute from there.
- It is a good example of an urban community in the age of globalisation: its social relationships are deepened and stretched by the imperatives of international communication.

Study Point

Discuss the strengths and weaknesses of the view that an airport is a good example of an urban community.

COMMUNITY: NEWLY NETWORKED

Sudjic (1992) has also argued that the concept of 'community' is too often used inappropriately: that there is an assumption of the 'natural' order of urban organisation and it is one based on the village or the small town, only writ large.

Like nationalists in search of the golden age when their nation was, as it were, 'top dog', so the idea of community is used to construct notions of fully integrated residential areas of extended kin, where everybody knows everybody else and where social problems are handled within the family, the church or by the local community leaders. Globalisation has clearly done little to challenge notions of the rural idyll and the community ideal.

Acculturation and the 'end' of the nation-state have, to a degree, undermined regional and national distinctiveness, but these trends have also worked in the opposite direction:

- Good-lifers continue to seek out the countryside to reclaim or to find *Gemeinschaft*.
- The networked society has enabled them to do so. Fax, electronic mail, the home photocopier, the cellular phone – all have facilitated economic activity outside the workplace and urban centre.
- The rise and rise of heritage and tourism is indicative of the search for a 'world we have lost'. Farm tourism presents the countryside to the urbanite in a safely-packaged form. The national stereotype has taken up its irony and added fun to its appeal. We laugh at beefeater dolls, but can we resist them when the cost is less than a pound, however ironic we think we are being?
- Gentrification and the ideology of the garden city have been the creative forces of community in the face of modern urban anomie. The reality of Bethnal Green may have been lost, but still the search for community goes on in the cities, in commuter and cathedral towns, and in the redevelopment of decayed inner city areas and docks.

NATION: RETURNING TO *GEMEINSCHAFT* AND *GESELLSCHAFT*

We have clearly not lost our stereotypes of the rural idyll, nor have we lost them in our characterisation of other nations. Globalisation has merged many cultures into one common denominator; it has forced our nation-states to be subservient to the political and economic will of others. Yet still we use simple binary opposites to understand ourselves: 'us' and 'them' defines our national identity in any age. This is an ideological construction not a reality, and for the Celts, for example, this was manifest in a caricature of themselves *vis-à-vis* the 'Anglo-Saxon' English (McCrone 1998):

In the words of McCrone, 'What we are dealing with here are not simple caricatures but antinomies of *Gemeinschaft* and *Gesellschaft* familiar to sociologists following Tönnies in which the former symbolised an organically bounded community, and the latter a mechanistically organised society'.

Table 16: *National Characteristics: 'Us and Them'*	
CELT	ANGLO-SAXON
feminine	masculine
community	society
feeling	reason
nature	culture
left	right

SOURCE: MCCRONE, 1998

Points of Evaluation

1   Globalisation forces us to consider what we may be losing; it concentrates the mind on national identity and the state of the nation.

2   Indeed, globalisation is often irrelevant to wider social inequalities which may be of greater immediacy. Race and gender inequalities can be eased by European legislation, yet that is no help 'out in the street' where dominant attitudes feed on cultures with long lineage.

3   The economic inequality resulting from the international division of labour, and national resistance to acculturation from the Japanese and American cores, demonstrates that the mobilising power of nationalism is as relevant to our everyday lives and the construction of our social selves as ever before. The nation-state may be splintering, but the nation retains its vibrancy.

WORLD CITIES, WORLD COMMUNITIES, WORLD NATIONS

Globalisation, then, has altered fundamentally the *relationships* between nations, between cities and between communities. We have long operated within an interconnected capitalist system, but it is perhaps the speed, cheapness and availability of a range of forms of communication which have made this process such a fundamental challenge to our understanding of who we are.

Activity
Read the extract below from Mitchell Moss. Then write 100–200 words on the changes we are now experiencing in the interrelationship between the city, the nation and the supranational organisation.

Communications technology, by extending the global reach of cities that are centres of information-based services, also affects the relationship of a city to its home nation. The world information capitals increasingly resemble the 'city states' of ancient Greece, for their density is remarkably independent of their own domestic economies. Such cities are intricately linked to each other through sophisticated telecommunications networks that operate on a round-the-clock basis. The face-to face activities that occur in these cities have not been made obsolete by new technology, rather, technology has extended the geographic reach of the individuals and the firms than transact the business in these world capitals. The operational boundaries of a city are no longer defined by geography of law, but by the reach of phone lines and computer networks. As McLuhan (1964) stated, 'a speed-up in communications always enables a central authority to extend its operations to more distant margins'.

...Population size was critical to city growth when the purpose of the city was to provide large numbers of labourers to work in the factories devoted to the manufacture and assembly of goods: today, the location of foreign banks, number of long distance telephones calls, and penetration of fax machines may be a more appropriate barometer of a city's economic health and vitality.

(Moss 'Telecommunications, world cities and urban policy', *Urban Studies*, 24, 1987)

SUMMARY

In this final chapter we have tried to demonstrates the challenge of globalisation to locality, community and nation. But rather than taking this to be the end of our story, we should perceive it as a new phase in how we interact with one another and with our rural and urban localities. Satellite and cable television companies offering banking, telephoning, home shopping and more, are already in many homes. Modems and links to the WWW are becoming common, although most use the Web at their place of work or at Internet cafes or public libraries. Sitting in front of a terminal is, of course, one of the most private and anomic experiences of the modern age, but it also opens up the opportunity for new levels of communication and, in particular, of information processing. This translates our notion of community into one free from the physical boundary of, say, Gosforth or Pentrediwaith, yet it creates new interactions in a way the city of the Chicago School could never have hoped to match. The general anonymity of relationships conducted over the Internet is countered by their frequency, reach and, in many cases, their continuity. These new networked communications are reminiscent of Wirth's assocational response to the anomic city, but at a level which has broken the constraints of physical locality and time.

National identity, too, has been reinvigorated. While the nation-state has found its sovereignty to be under challenge, it has been the nation and national identity which has been the beneficiary. *How* a people are governed has been historically less relevant than being governed equally and satisfactorily (Morton 1996a). As citizenship evolves in a world of supranational organisations, it is inevitable that loyalty to a state is fragmented: but that does not weaken the power of the national idea to mobilise and homogenise opinion. Throughout this book we have stressed that the British nation-state has contained four civil societies, those of its constituent nations. We have also stressed that the many ethnic groups which have gained citizenship of Britain add to the sense of inadequacy with a singular 'British' identity. What our discussion of globalisation has contributed further is that we should expect the hybridity of national identity to continue. Competing and complementary national identities are products of competing and complementary localities and their communities.

STUDY GUIDE

Group work

Our final suggestion for group work returns to the themes of locality, community and nation. In this chapter some ways in which these three concepts have changed in the age of globalisation have been suggested. Now work to see what you can add to our list.

Divide into three groups, each to take either locality, community or nation as its theme. Seeking your evidence through the World Wide Web would be appropriate so use it to find instances of changes in locality, community and nation. We have given some indications of the WWW addresses that may be of use throughout the text and have added to them in the resource section at the end of this book. The NISS information gateway is a good place to try first. Alternatively, try one of the internet search engines. Two of the most popular are Yahoo! (http://www.yahoo.com) and Excite (http://www.excite.com).

Coursework

Test the hypothesis that a 'networked community' is just as real as the communities studied by Williams, Frankenberg, Littlejohn and Young and Willmott. Without subscribing to a user group that costs any money, and if you have permission, try to join and/or observe the communications attached to certain groups using the World Wide Web. You could log in to a fan club, a classical literature discussion group, a political society or group concerned with current affairs. Do these groups in themselves, or collectively, recreate the 'community ideal' in the networked age? On completion of your search, discuss whether we should now reconceptualise the community through the World Wide Web as the prime carrier and creator of social relationship, of culture and of commerce?

The meaning of globalisation, its effects on the nation-state and on national identity are the most relevant questions likely to be asked. You might also be asked to analyse the changes in locality and community as a result of the new challenges of globalisation. A possible question might be:

Will the globalisation process destroy the nation-state for good?

Some of the themes you could include are: a definition of globalisation; some threats to the nation-state; some possible consequences of globalisation; the difficulty in creating a pan-European identity; the continued significance of national identities; whether globalisation is over-stated as a concept.

From this chapter, you should now understand the following themes. Take time to make a key concept card on each:

- A definition of globalisation.
- The challenge of globalisation to the nation-state and to national identity.
- The stretching and deepening of time, breaking the geopolitical constraints of the community.
- The possible consequences of globalisation: homogenisation, local particularism, hybridity in identity.
- Whether globalisation is over-stated as a concept.
- The continued significance of the binary opposites of *Gemeinschaft* and *Gesellschaft*, rural and urban, 'us' and 'them', to how locality, community and nation are popularly perceived.
- The networked society; a new version of 'community' in the global village.

1 Explain and assess the claim that 'the global village is now a reality'. How has this affected the significance of the concepts of locality and community?
2 How valid is the concept of a 'networked community' in an age when new technology has changed relationship in most areas of society, and provided new global opportunities to communicate instantly with others?

FURTHER READING, RESOURCES AND BIBLIOGRAPHY

An appropriate starting place for those just developing their interests around the themes of locality, community and nation would be the Reader produced by Bell and Newby (1974). This contains extracts from the most influential community studies and the best discussion of *Gemeinschaft* and *Gesellschaft* by Elias. For a literary approach, see Raymond Williams (1960) *Border Country*, London: Penguin. See also his *The Country and the City* (1973) London: Hogarth. A good theoretical understanding of locality and community in an urban setting can be found in Dilys M. Hill (1994) *Citizens and Cities: urban policy in the 1990s*, London: Harvester Wheatsheaf.

A straightforward guide to recent trends in British culture is contained in Bassnett (1997), while Gilroy (1987) is the best introduction to Afro-Caribbean culture in Britain. Kettle and Hodge (1982) provide a great deal of contemporary source material in their discussion of the race riots in Britain in the 1980s; for race and housing see S.J. Smith (1989).

To understand the 'postmodern' city and urban landscape see Sudjic (1992) and Garreau (1988); for urban statistics see OECD (1996). The best historical accounts of the industrial city, of which all contain discussion of urban planning in the twentieth century, are Sutcliffe (1981), Waller (1983), and R.J. Morris and R. Rodger (eds) (1993) *The Victorian City, 1820–1914: A Reader in British Urban History*, London: Longman.

The issue of nationalism is well served by a multidisciplinary Reader containing extracts from the classic texts: Hutchinson and Smith (1994). By far the best discussion of nationalism from a purely sociological standpoint is found in McCrone (1998). Three thought-provoking accounts of Englishness/Britishness are Wiener (1981), Taylor (1991) and Philip Dodd (1995) *The Battle over Britain*, London: Demos. A valuable source book on literary reflections of Englishness is J. Giles and T. Middleton (eds) (1995) *Writing Englishness: 1900–1950*, London: Routledge. For Scottish nationalism see McCrone (1992); historically, see Morton (1998b) and M. Lynch (ed.) (1993) *Scotland, 1850–1979: Society, Politics and Union*, London: The Historical Association. For Ireland, see Downing (1980) and Boyce (1996): for Wales, Osmond (1988) and Evans (1989).

To understand uneven development in the wider world, see Webster (1984) and for its urban context, A.D. King (1990) *Global Cities*, London: Routledge. Globalisation is best understood from Hall, Held and McGrew (1992) and D. Held (1995) *Democracy and the Global Order*, Cambridge: Polity.

RESOURCES

There is a range of videos which are commercially available or which can be borrowed from some of the specialised archives. We recommend the following:

- *Port Sunlight, 1931*, reels 2 and 3 (reference VT 1116). This films shows employees leaving the factory for Port Sunlight village: its 'country-style' cottages, leisure activities, village hall, healthcare and other features of enlightened employer housing provision.
- *A City Speaks: Hulme 1946*. This five-minute extract concentrates on plans to redevelop Hulme and compares housing conditions there with the Wythenshawe estate, in *Moving Memories 4* (commercially available).
- A second film on these estates can be found on *Moving Memories 2* (commercially available), in addition to *The changing face of Salford: life in the slums 1969*.

All are produced by the North West Film Archive, Manchester Metropolitan University, Minshull House, 47–49 Chorlton Street, Manchester M1 3EU (See also: http://www.mmu.ac.uk/services/library/nwfa/). Their services are free to the higher education sector, but some requests might incur a fee, and copyright restrictions apply.

Although a little dated, a useful list of films on Northern Ireland can be found in T. Downing (ed.) (1980) *The Troubles*, London: Thames Television/Futura. For Scotland, the BBC's recently updated *Restless Nation* series, and accompanying book (Edinburgh: Mainstream 1997), is very perceptive, with a good range of visual material for the period since 1945.

There are many films produced on the British monarchy, but Panorama (17 November 1997, BBC 1) is insightful. On the 'rural idyll', see: B.P. McLaughlin (1983) *Country crisis: the lid off the chocolate box*, produced by Television South West for Channel 4 Plymouth: Channel Four Television.

WWW

In addition to the World Wide Web addresses given throughout the text, here are some useful points of contact for further sociological enquiry:

- NISS Information Gateway: http://www.niss.ac.uk/
- Sociological Research On-Line:
  http://www.socresonline.org.uk/socresonline/
- CCTA Government Information Service: htt://www.open.gov.uk/

- Scottish Local Government: maps, key statistics and contact addresses/telephone numbers etc.:
http://www.trp.dundee.ac.uk/data/councils/ncintro.html
- SOCINFO web site: http://www.stir.ac.uk/socinfo/
- Social Science Information Gateway: http://www.sosig.ac.uk/
- Social Research Update: http://www.soc.surrey.ac.uk/sru.html
- Political Studies Association (PSA): http://www.lgu.ac.uk/psa/psa.html
- Centre for Applied Social Survey: Social and community planning research:
http://www.scpr.ac.uk/cass/
- Economic and Social Research Council: Data Archive:
http://dawww.essex.ac.uk/
- British official publications current awareness service (BOPCAS):
http://www.soton.ac.uk/~nukop/index.html
- Office for National Statistics: http://main.emap.com/ons97/
- United States Census Bureau: http://www.census.gov/
- 'Urban Sprawl': http://riceinfo.rice.edu/~Ida/Sprawl_Net/

BIBLIOGRAPHY

Abrams, P. (1978) 'Towns and Economic Growth', in P. Abrams & E.A. Wrigley (eds) *Towns in Societies*. Cambridge: Cambridge University Press.

Allanson, P. & Whitby, M. (1996) *The Rural Economy and the British Countryside*. London: Earthscan.

Anderson, B. (1991) *Imagined Communities*. London: Verso.

Badcock, B. (1984) *Unfairly Structures Cities*. Oxford: Basil Blackwell.

Bassnett, S. (ed.) (1997) *Studying British Cultures: An Introduction*. London: Routledge.

Bell, C. & Newby, H. (1971) *Community Studies: An Introduction to the Sociology of the Local Community*. London: Allen & Unwin.

Bell, C & Newby, H. (eds) (1974) *The Sociology of Community: A Selection of Readings*. London: Cass.

Bell, C., Newby, H., Saunders P. & Rose, D. (1978) *Property, Paternalism and Power: Class and Control in rural England*. London: Hutchinson.

Billig, M. (1995) *Banal Nationalism*. London: Sage.

Boyce, D.G. (1996) *The Irish Question and British Politics, 1868–1996*, 2nd ed. Basingstoke: Macmillan.

Braudel, F. (1974) *Capitalism and Material Life, 1400–1800*, trans. by M. Kochan. London: Fontana.

Braudel, F. (1985) *The Structures of Everyday Life*, trans. S. Reynolds. London: Fontana.

Brown, A., McCrone D. & Paterson L. (1996) *Politics and Society in Scotland.* London: Macmillian.

Cannadine, D. (1983) 'The context, performance and meaning of ritual: the British monarchy and the 'invention of tradition', c. 1820–1977', in Hobsbawm & Ranger (eds) *The Invention of Tradition.* Cambridge: Canto.

Cashmore, E.E. (1989) *United Kingdom?: Class, Race and Gender since the War.* London: Unwin Hyman.

Cohen, A.P. (1987) *Whalsay: Symbol, Segment and Boundary in a Shetland Island Community.* Manchester: Manchester University Press.

Cohen, A.P. (ed.) (1982) *Belonging: Identity and Social Organisation in British Rural Cultures.* Manchester: Manchester University Press.

Colley, L. (1992) *Britons.* London: Yale University Press.

Coupland, A. (1992) 'Docklands: dream or disaster', in A. Thornley (ed.) *The Crisis of London.* London: Routledge.

Cowan, H. (1990) 'Regency icons: marketing Cheltenham's built environment', in M. Harloe, C.G. Pickvance & J. Urry (eds) *Place, Policy and Politics. Do Localities Matter?* London: Unwin Hyman.

Crick, B. (1989) 'An Englishman considers his passport', in Evans (ed.) *National Identity in the British Isles.* Coleg Harlech Occasional Papers in Welsh Studies, No. 3.

Davis, K. (1974) 'The urbanisation of the human population', in C. Tilly (ed.) *An Urban World.* Boston: Little Brown.

Davis, M. (1994) *Beyond Blade Runner: Urban Control, the Ecology of Fear.* New Jersey: Open Magazine Pamphlet Series.

Dyos, H.J. & Reeder, D. (1973) 'Slums and Suburbs', in H.J. Dyos & M. Woolf (eds) *The Victorian City.* London: Routledge & Kegan Paul.

Elias, N. (1974) 'Foreword' in C. Bell & H. Newby (eds) *The Sociology of Community: A Selection of Readings.* London: Cass.

Evans, N. (ed.) (1989) *National Identity in the British Isles*, Coleg Harlech Occasional Papers in Welsh Studies, No. 3.

Fujita, K. (1991) 'A World City and Flexible Specialisation: restructuring the Tokyo metropolis', *International Journal of Urban and Regional Research*, **15**, 2, June.

Galpin, C.J. (1920) *Rural Life.* New York: The Centuary Company.

Garreau, J. (1988) *Edge City.* New York: Anchor Books.

Gellner, E. (1983) *Nations and Nationalism.* Oxford: Basil Blackwell.

Giddens, A. (1985) *A Contemporary Critique of Historical Materialism Vol. II.* London: Polity.

Giddens, A. (1990) *The Consequences of Modernity.* London: Polity.

Gilroy, P. (1992) *'There ain't no black in the Union Jack'.* London: Routledge.

Gilroy, P. (1996) 'One Nation under a Groove: the Cultural Politics of "Race" and Racism in Britain', in G. Eley and R.G. Suny (eds) *Becoming National: A Reader.* Oxford: Oxford University Press.

Hall, S. (1992) 'The question of cultural identity', in S. Hall, D. Held & A. McGrew (eds) *Modernity and its Futures.* Cambridge: Polity Press.

Held, D. (1996) 'The decline of the nation-state', in G. Eley and R.G Suny (eds) *Becoming National: A Reader.* Oxford: Oxford University Press.

Heller, A. (1989) *Everyday Life.* London: Routledge & Kegan Paul.

Hobsbawm, E.J. (1992) *Nations and Nationalism since 1780.* Cambridge: Canto.

Housman, A.E. (1939) *The Collected Poems of A.E. Housman.* London: Jonathan Cape.

Hutchinson, J. & Smith, A.D. (eds) (1994) *Nationalism.* Oxford: Oxford University Press.

Jacobson, J. (1997) 'Perceptions of Britishness', *Nations and Nationalism*, **3**, 2.

Jarvie, G. & Walker G. (eds) (1994) *Scottish Sport in the Making of the Nation: Ninety Minute Patriots?* Leicester: Leicester University Press.

Jones, G.E. (1973) *Rural Life: Patterns and Processes.* London: Longman.

Kellas, J.G. (1984) *The Scottish Political System*, 3rd ed. Cambridge: Cambridge University Press.

Kohn, H. (1940) 'The Genesis and Character of English nationalism', *Journal of the History of Ideas.*

Kohn, H. (1946) *Prophets and Peoples.* New York: Macmillan.

Kolb, J.H. (1921) 'Rural Primary Groups', *Research Bulletin*, 51.

Ley, D. (1983) *A Social Geography of the City.* New York: Harper & Row.

MacNee, K. (1996) 'Living in Rural Scotland: a study of life in four rural communities'. Edinburgh: The Scottish Office Central Research Unit.

Mann, M. (1996) 'Nation-states in Europe and other countries: Diversifying, developing, not dying', in G. Balakrishnan (ed.) *Mapping the nation.* London: Verso.

McCrone, D. (1992) *Understanding Scotland: the sociology of a stateless nation.* London: Routledge.

McCrone, D. (1997) 'Land, Democracy and Culture in Scotland', The Fourth McEwan Lecture on Land Tenure in Scotland, Rural Forum: Perth.

McCrone, D. (1998) *Tomorrow's Ancestors: the Sociology of Nationalism.* London: Routledge.

McCrone, D., Morris, A. Kiely, R. (1995) *Scotland – the Brand: The Making of Scottish Heritage.* Edinburgh: Edinburgh University Press.

McGrew, A. (1992) 'A global society?' in S. Hall, D. Held & A. McGrew (eds) *Modernity and its Futures.* Cambridge: Polity Press.

Mclaughlin, B. (1985) 'Deprivation in rural areas', unpublished report to the Department of Environment.

Midwinter, A. & Monghan, C. (1990) 'The Measurement & Analysis of Rural Deprivation'. Report prepared for COSLA: Edinburgh.

Miller, A. (1980) 'A Study of Multiply-deprived Households in Scotland', Report, Central Research Unit, Scottish Office: Edinburgh.

Mingay, G. (ed.) (1989) *The Rural Idyll,* London: Routledge.

Modood, T. (1994) 'Political Blackness and British Asians', *Sociology,* **28**, 4.

Morris, A. & Gladstone, J. (1997) 'The Role of Farm Tourism and Agricultural Heritage in the Social and Economic Regeneration of Rural Scotland', Report to The Scottish Office Agriculture, Environment, & Fisheries Department: Edinburgh.

Morris, A. (1994) 'Rural Sociology: The Poor Relation?', *The Social Science Teacher* (Summer).

Morris, R.J. (1990) 'Externalities, the market, power structures and the urban agenda', *Urban History Yearbook,* **17**.

Morton, G. (1996a) 'Scottish rights and 'centralisation' in the mid-nineteenth century', *Nations and Nationalism,* **2**, 2.

Morton, G. (1996b) 'Review Essay: Sir William Wallace and other tall stories (unlikely mostly)', *Scottish Affairs,* **14**, Spring.

Morton, G. (1998a) 'What if … ? The significance of Scotland's 'missing' nationalism in the nineteenth century', in D. Broun, R. Finlay & M. Lynch (eds) *Image and Identity: the making and remaking of Scotland through the ages.* Edinburgh: John Donald.

Morton, G. (1998b) *Unionist-Nationalism: Governing Urban Scotland, 1830–1860.* East Linton: Tuckwell Press.

Nairn, T. (1981) *The Break-up of Britain,* 2nd edn. London: Verso.

Nairn, T. (1988) *The Enchanted Glass: Britain and its Monarchy.* London: Hutchinson.

Newby, H. (1985) *The Countryside in Question.* London: Hutchinson.

Nisbet, R. (1967) *The Sociological Tradition.* London: Heinemann.

OECD (1996) *Strategies for Housing and Social Interaction in Cities.* Paris: Organisation for Economic Co-operation and Development.

Palen, J.J. & London, B. (1984) *Gentrification, Displacement and Neighbourhood Revitalisation.* Albany: State University of New York Press.

Park, R.E. *et al.* (1925) *The City.* Chicago: University of Chicago Press.

Reissman, L. (1964) *The Urban Process*. New York/London: The Free Press of Glencoe.

Ritzer, G. (1996) *The McDonaldization of Society*, revised edition. California: Pine Forge Press.

Rogers, A. (1989) 'A Planned Countryside', in Mingay (ed.) *The Rural Idyll*. London: Routledge.

Ross, E. (1983), 'Survival Networks: Women's neighbourhood sharing in London before World War I', *History Workshop Jounrnal*.

Shils, E. (1995) 'Nation, nationality, nationalism and civil society'. *Nations and Nationalism*, **1**, 1, March.

Shucksmith, M., Chapman, P. Clark, G. & Black, S. (1994) 'Disadvantage in Rural Scotland': Summary Report to Rural Forum: Perth.

Sklair, L. (1995) 'Social Movements and Global Capitalism', *Sociology*, **29**, 3.

Smith, A.D. (1986) *The Ethnic Origin of Nations*. Oxford: Blackwell.

Smith, A.D. (1991) *National Identity*. London: Penguin.

Smith, A.D. (1995) *Nations and Nationalism in a Global Era*. Cambridge: Polity Press.

Smith, S.J. (1989) *The Politics of 'Race' and Residence*. Cambridge: Polity Press.

Sudjic, D. (1992) *The 100 Mile City*. London: Andre Deutsch.

Sutcliffe, A. (1981) *Towards the planned city*. Oxford: Basil Blackwell.

Taylor, P.J. (1991) 'The English and their Englishness: 'a curious, mysterious, elusive and little understood people", *Scottish Geographical Magazine*, **107**, 3.

Waller, P.J. (1983) *Town, City and Nation: England, 1850–1914*. Oxford: Oxford University Press.

Weber, M. (1958) *The City*, trans. D. Martindale & G. Newwirth. London: The Free Press.

Webster, A. (1984) *Introduction to the Sociology of Development*. London: Macmillan.

Wiener, M.J. (1981) *English Culture and the Decline of the Industrial Spirit, 1850–1980*. London: Pelican.

Wirth, L. (1938) 'Urbanism as a way of life', *American Journal of Sociology*, 44.

Woolf, S. (ed.) (1996) *Nationalism in Europe: 1815 to the present*. London: Routledge.

Yearley, S. (1991) *The Green Case*. London: HarperCollins Academic.

INDEX